"I Made It Myself"

40 Kids Craft Projects

Alan & Gill Bridgewater

TAB BOOKS

Blue Ridge Summit, PA

DEDICATION
Thank you Gyln—
Thank you Julian—
We couldn't have managed
without your help.

FIRST EDITION
FIRST PRINTING

Library of Congress Cataloging-in-Publication Data

Bridgewater, Alan.
   ''I made it myself'' : 40 kids' craft projects / by Alan and Gill
Bridgewater.
    p.   cm.
   Summary: Gives instructions for making a variety of toys and games from easily available materials.
   ISBN 0-8306-8339-9   ISBN 0-8306-3339-1 (pbk.)
   1. Handicraft—Juvenile literature. [1. Handicraft. 2. Toy
making.]   I. Bridgewater, Gill. II. Title.
TT157.B745 1990
745.592—dc20   89-49450
                                CIP

TAB BOOKS offers software for sale. For information and a catalog, please contact TAB Software Department, Blue Ridge Summit, PA 17294-0850.

Questions regarding the content of this book should be addressed to:

   Reader Inquiry Branch
   TAB BOOKS
   Blue Ridge Summit, PA 17294-0214

Acquisitions Editor: Kimberly Tabor
Book Editor: Joanne M. Slike
Production: Katherine G. Brown
Book Design: Jaclyn J. Boone

Contents

Introduction

KIDS LOVE CRAFTS! Snipping with scissors, folding crisp brightly colored papers, carefully mounting and sticking card cutouts, twisting and bending wire, turning cotton reels into wheels and beads into washers, using beautiful soft-haired brushes to lay on thick juicy slurps of brightly colored paint and spreading oozy sticks of glue—"*I Made It Myself*": *40 Kids' Crafts Projects* is all of these and much, much more.

This book is about all the joyful hands-on pleasures of using craft tools and everyday materials. We will show you how to make lots of really wonderful fun projects. And don't think that the fun is only in the doing; once made, our projects become exciting and stimulating objects in their own right. Okay, so you might not go much on the printed wrapping paper or the greeting card, but then again, think how good it will feel when your mom or grandma receives a present that you have made—just wait until you see the look of pleasure on your mom or grandmother's face!

Many of the projects in this book are toys and games for kids. A wind racer yacht, a matchbox dancer, a cat's eye pocket game, a glider, a kite, a climbing clown, a set of drums, a moon mask, a whistle, a cowboy lantern, a pony-tail game, a water bomb—they are all great fun.

Just think of it, not only will you be able to sample all the finger-tingling, cutting and folding, sticking and painting delights of making the crafts, you will also be able to use and play with the projects knowing that, if it weren't for you, they would still be just bits and pieces of glue, cardboard, and plastic.

Don't worry if you are all fingers and thumbs, we will show you the way. With all the projects being carefully thought out as a series of linked steps, and with our problem-solving lists, cautions, watch-points, and follow-ups, we have made sure that each and every stage is as smooth and as easy as possible. But don't get me wrong, the projects aren't so easy that they aren't worth doing; each project is without doubt a good-fun challenge. And remember, by the time you have worked through the projects, you will be a kids' crafts egghead—a kids' crafts genius!

So there you are. Talk the projects out with your parents, decide how you want the designs to be adjusted to suit your tools and materials, spend time scrounging around the house looking for suitable throwaway junk items, clear a worksurface, and then roll up your sleeves and get ready for action.

Of course at the end of the day, your glider might do several loops and make a wild crash landing into your dad's favorite flower bed, and yes, the whistle might not whistle and the water bomb might just bounce back and give you a soaking. But even so, the gliders, kites, dolls, clowns, bangs and whistles (WOW! SPLISH! SPLASH!) are all a wonderful part of the wonderful kids' crafts experience. Best of luck!

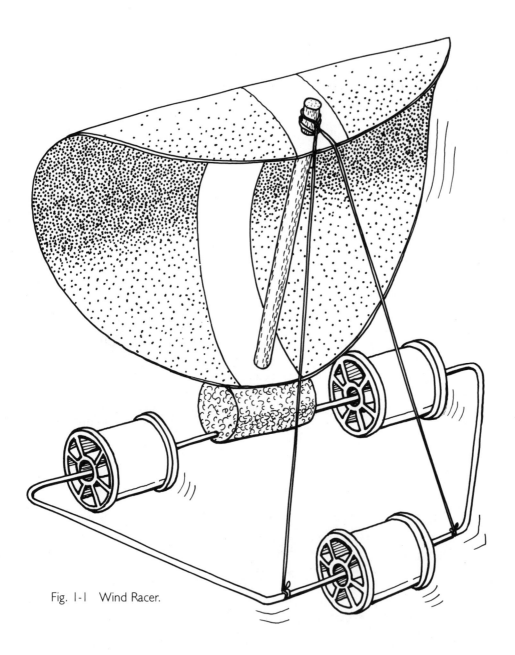

Fig. 1-1 Wind Racer.

Wind Racer
A wind racer land-yacht toy

Wind-filled sails billowing and taut, and the smooth soft swish-swish-swish as the wind slices the yacht forward through the water, sailing is a really exciting pastime. Okay, so you don't own a yacht, or maybe you live about a thousand miles away from the nearest large stretch of water, but have you ever tried sand-yacht or land-yacht racing? You still have a mast and wind-filled sails, the only difference is that instead of having a boat and water, you have a buggy, wheels, and dry land.

Our wind racer land yacht toy is a speedy smooth-mover. Wait for a windy day, put it down on a smooth surface—perhaps a school playground or a tennis court—and then stand back and watch the fun. When the wind catches the sails, off she goes, just a soft silent glide as the wheels turn and the yacht moves forward. Beautiful!

MAKING TIME AND SKILL LEVEL

Although the various making stages are relatively easy, the sum total of all the stages makes the project just a little bit tricky. This project is best suited to older children or to an adult-child team. Bearing in mind that you will almost certainly have to modify the measurements to suit the sizes of your particular cork and thread spools, an 8- to 12-year-old should be able to make a working racer in about 20 to 30 minutes. But then again, if you want to make something extra-special, say, a yacht with fancy trim and go-faster stripes, then allow a couple of hours.

Cautions and adult help   Wire bending can be difficult. Best gather together all your tools and found materials and then ask an adult for help and advice.

Be warned   When you are working with wire and pliers, you do have to watch out for your eyes and your fingers. Plan out the bends, measure twice and cut once, and be careful that you don't nip your fingers in the pliers.

TOOLS AND MATERIALS

☐ A piece of thin coat hanger-type wire about 24 inches long
☐ Three plastic or wooden thread spools   ☐ A large fat wine bottle cork
☐ A thin dowel about 8 inches long
☐ A sheet of thin colored cardboard 9×9 inches
☐ A roll of masking tape   ☐ A pencil and ruler   ☐ A paper punch

Continued

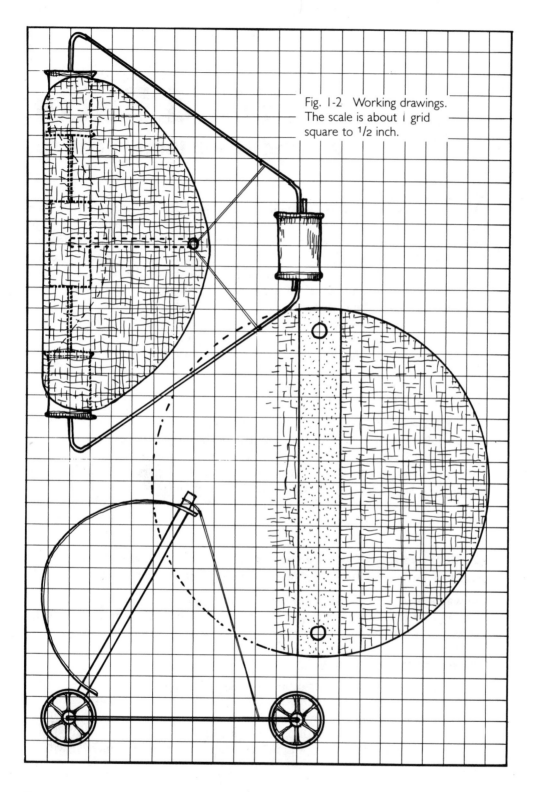

Fig. 1-2 Working drawings. The scale is about 1 grid square to 1/2 inch.

☐ A pair of long-nose pliers ☐ A length of thin cotton thread
☐ A tube of clear quick-set glue ☐ A compass/pair of compasses

MEASURE, MARK AND MAKE

1 Have a good long look at the project picture (FIG. 1-1), and the working draw-ing page (FIG. 1-2), and see how the yacht's chassis is made up from the thin wire and spools. See how the wire passes through the three spools and how its ends are pushed into the cork.

2 Because corks and spools come in all shapes and sizes, look at our design, and then have a tryout with the pliers and scrap wire.

3 Aim for a wide, low, four-sided shape with easy, smooth bends, and with the holes in the cork down low and well off-center. Spike the dowel mast into the cork so that it angles back, and attach with a dab of clear glue (FIG. 1-3).

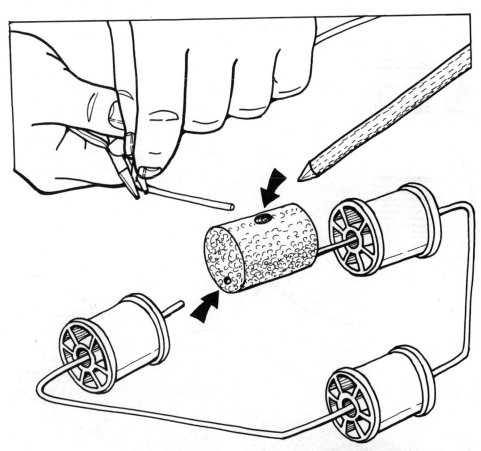

Fig. 1-3 (Top Left) Use the pliers to bend the wire, then thread up on the spools. (Bottom) Push the wire end into the bottom edge of the cork, one end on each side.

4 When you come to making the sail, draw an 8-inch-diameter circle on the thin colored cardboard and then cut out with scissors.

5 Strengthen the sail disk by running a length of masking tape right round the card, then punch in the two mast holes. Set the holes about 1/2 inch back from the edge of the card (FIG. 1-4 top).

6 Slide the sail on the mast.

7 Finally, brace the sail by looping the cotton thread over the top of the mast and running it down and tying it to the wire chassis.

WATCH-POINTS AND FOLLOW-UPS

○ You could use this toy as a prototype and then make a full-size sit-on racer. Ask an adult to help.
○ When you are spiking holes in the cork, be careful that the cork doesn't split open.
○ You could experiment with different-shape sails and mast heights.
○ You could look at books on dinghy sailing.

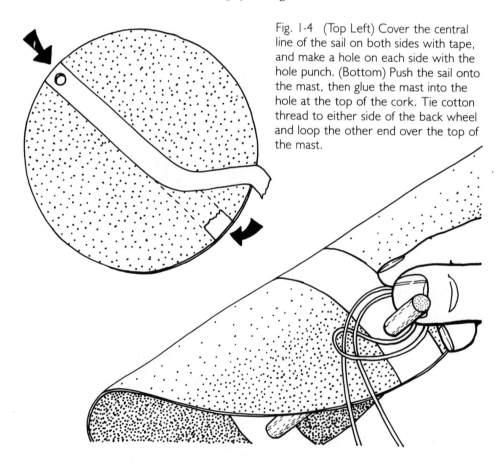

Fig. 1-4 (Top Left) Cover the central line of the sail on both sides with tape, and make a hole on each side with the hole punch. (Bottom) Push the sail onto the mast, then glue the mast into the hole at the top of the cork. Tie cotton thread to either side of the back wheel and loop the other end over the top of the mast.

Dizzy Dancer
A dancing doll

A baby doll to cuddle, a teddy bear to kiss, a large walking, talking doll to take for walks—most of us have, at some time or other, enjoyed playing with a doll-type toy. If you like dolls, you are going to like this project.

Our Dizzy Dancer is so pretty. She will dance and dance and dance the night away. With her beautiful red and white lacy dress, her delicate long arms and smooth, dark hair, she could well be a Spanish señorita. And as for her dancing, her little feet are so light and her steps are so springy that they look to be whirling and twirling around. Our dancer is a beautiful toy—she's easy to make and she's fun. Hold her around the waist, run her backwards and forwards on the carpet, and watch her little feet dance round and round and round. . . .

MAKING TIME AND SKILL LEVEL

An easy-to-make delightful, good-fun project, an 8- to 12-year-old will be able to make the dancer in about 50 minutes.

Cautions and adult help Although all the making stages are easy enough, putting the doll together can be a bit tricky. If you think that you can go it alone, fine. If not, ask an older brother or sister or an adult for help.

Be warned All tools and materials are potentially dangerous—scissors, pencils, rulers, sticky tape, plastics and adhesives. If you use them in the wrong way, there is a chance that you might hurt yourself.

Be extra careful when you are using the scissors. Watch out for your fingers, your eyes, your baby brothers and sisters, and your pets. If you don' t really know how to use a pair of scissors, ask an adult to show you how.

TOOLS AND MATERIALS

- ☐ A couple of sheets of cardboard—thick cardboard for the main figure and thinner cardboard for the skirt sides and the wheel
- ☐ A sheet of tracing paper   ☐ A pencil and ruler
- ☐ A tin/tube of paper/card adhesive   ☐ A pair of scissors
- ☐ A couple of brushes, one broad and the other fine-point.
- ☐ A hole punch   ☐ A brass fold-tab clip.
- ☐ A scrap cut from a smooth throwaway plastic lid
- ☐ A few inches of masking tape   ☐ A plastic drinking straw

MEASURE, MARK AND MAKE

I Have a long careful look at the project picture (FIG. 2-1) and the pattern page (FIG. 2-2). Note the three-thickness construction, the way the wheel pivots inside the dress, and the way the dress is trimmed with a paper doily.

2 When you have studied all the construction details, trace off the four shapes that make up the project, and carefully pencil-press-transfer the traced lines through to the cardboard. There should be four shapes in all: the main dress-head-and-shoulders cut from the thick cardboard, and the two dress sides and legs-wheel cut from the thin cardboard.

Continued

Fig. 2-1 Dizzy Dancer.

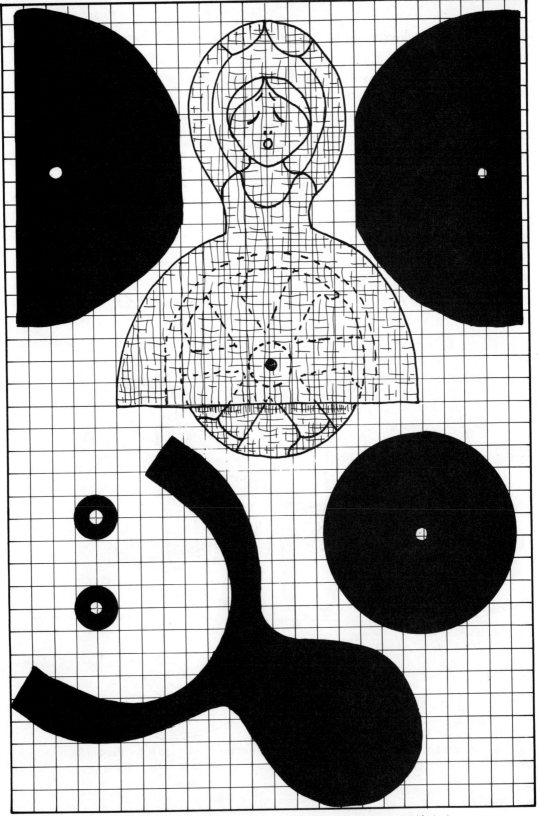

Fig. 2-2 Working drawing. The scale is about 1 grid square to 1/4 inch.

3 Cut two small disks from the thin plastic and work them with the paper punch to make two washers.

4 Mark in the pivot points on the wheel and the two dress sides, then carefully press the holes through with the punch.

5 Stick the half-circle dresses on each side of the main form (FIG. 2-3 bottom)

6 When the glue is dry, block in the main areas of color, pick out the details with a fine-point brush and black paint (FIG. 2-3 top).

7 Push the feet-wheel up inside the dress slide the two washers in on each side of the wheel. Make sure that all pivotal holes are aligned (FIG. 2-4 bottom).

8 Cut a narrow strip of masking tape and wrap it around and around the brass tab-clip. Cover the tape with a short length of plastic straw (FIG. 2-4 top)

9 Push the clip through the dress sides and the wheel, and bend the tabs down and over.

10 Finally, decorate the dress sides with scraps cut from the paper doily.

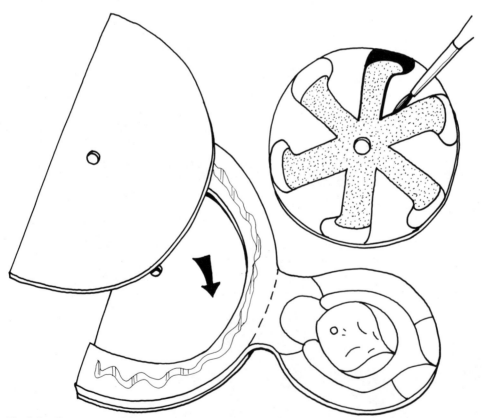

Fig. 2-3 (Bottom Left) Glue the skirts, one on each side of the figure. (Top Right) Paint in the main areas of colors. Finally, with a fine-point brush, outline and paint in the black areas.

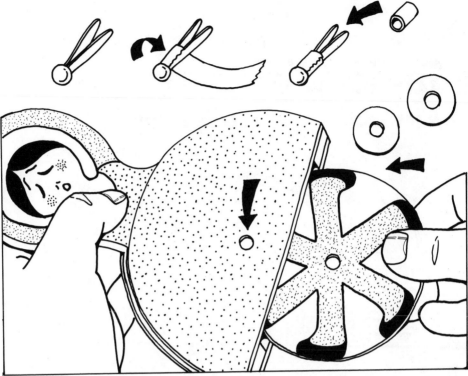

Fig. 2-4 (Top, left to right) Cover the paper clip by rolling tape around it. Then cover the tape with a small piece of straw. (Bottom) With a washer on each side of the leg circle, fit and align the holes and push the paper clip into position.

WATCH-POINTS AND FOLLOW-UPS

○ When you are choosing your cardboard, best go for a white-faced board

○ If you want to make a stronger dancer, you could use $1/8$- to $3/16$-inch-thick plywood rather than cardboard and then cut it—or ask an adult to cut it—using a coping saw. (*See* Glossary.)

3
Magic Disk
A Victorian thaumatrope toy

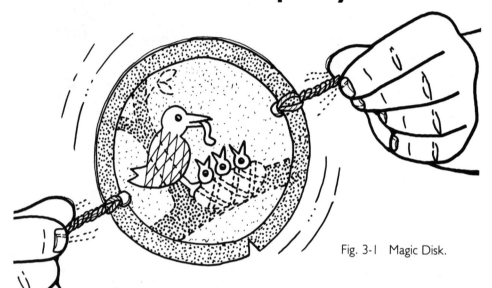

Fig. 3-1 Magic Disk.

The Victorians loved clever toys or scopes sometimes also called *tropes*. They had kaleidoscopes, stroboscopes, phenakistascopes, fantascopes, praxinoscopes, stereoscopes, and thaumatropes.

When our great-great grandparents first saw thaumatropes they were amazed and even a little frightened. Invented in about 1826, the thaumatrope or "magic disk," is really no more than a disk with pictures on both sides. The clever bit is that when the disk is spun, our eyes or brain sees both pictures as part of a single picture. For example, with our thaumatrope, when the disk is spun, the mother bird, worm, and little heads of the baby birds on one side of the disk get all mixed up with the tree and the nest on the other side of the card to make a complete scene. Now you see it, now you don't! Thaumatropes are really good fun.

MAKING TIME AND SKILL LEVEL

This is a very simple easy-to-make project. A disk of cardboard, a few minutes spent drawing, and the project is three-parts made. A 6- to 12-year-old should be able to make a passable thaumatrope in almost less time than it takes to blink. Plan on having it made in about 5 to 10 minutes.

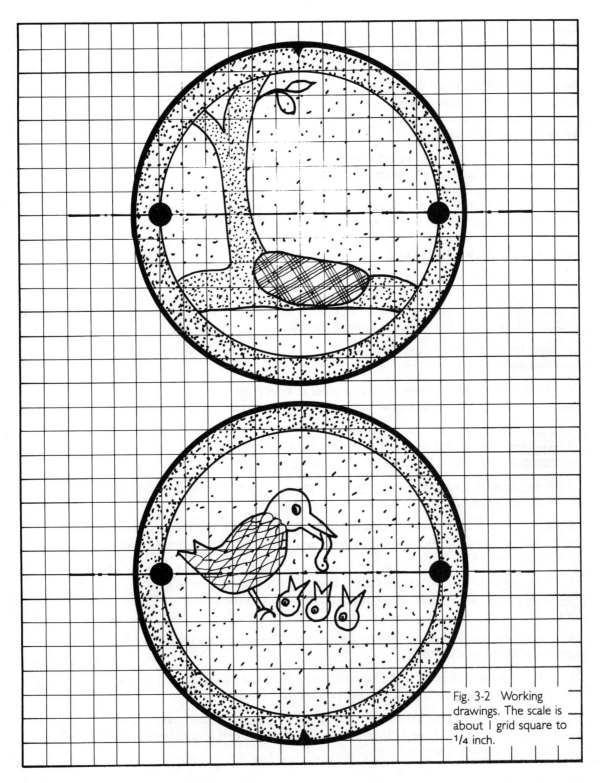

Fig. 3-2 Working drawings. The scale is about 1 grid square to ¹/₄ inch.

Cautions and adult help   This is one of those projects that can be changed to suit a child's age and ability. Although all the stages are safe enough, younger children might need help when they come to fixing the exact position of the pictures.

Be warned   Even a piece of spinning cardboard can be dangerous. Keep it away from you hair and away from your pets.

TOOLS AND MATERIALS

- ☐ A piece of stiff white-faced cardboard about 4×4 inches
- ☐ A sheet of tracing paper to fit the card
- ☐ A compass/pair of compasses   ☐ A pair of scissors
- ☐ A pencil and ruler   ☐ A pack of colored felt-tip pens   ☐ A hole punch
- ☐ A piece of knitting yarn or thin string about 36 inches long

MEASURE, MARK AND MAKE

1   Have a look at the project picture (FIG. 3-1) and the working drawing or pattern (FIG. 3-2) and note how the two pictures need to be drawn on each side of the disk. See how the drawings are placed in relationship to the punched holes, the centerlines and the little cut on the edge of the disk.

2   Take the 4×4-inch piece of white-faced cardboard and fix its center by drawing cross diagonals.

3   With the compass set to a radius or point-to-pencil distance of $1^3/_4$ inches, spike the point on the center of the cardboard and draw a clean-edged $3^1/_2$-inch-diameter circle.

4   Take the scissors and cut out the circle. Make a little scissor-nick on one of the diagonals, meaning at the edge of the circle.

5   With the scissor-nick placed at top-center, measure $1/_4$ inch in from each side of the disk and carefully punch out the two string holes.

6   With the card turned over so that the nick is at top-center, line the nest tracing up with the two spin holes and pencil-press-transfer the traced lines through to the card (FIG. 3-3 top).

7   Now, with the nick at bottom-center, line the bird tracing up with two spin-holes and pencil-press-transfer the traced lines through to the card (FIG. 3-3 bottom).

8   Use the felt-tip pens to color in the design (FIG. 3-3 top). Best outline the picture first with the black pen.

9   Cut the 36-inch piece of string into half, loop and knot each half, and finally loop and knot the string through the disk holes (FIG. 3-4 top).

10   Finally, to work the magic disk, wind it up by tossing it over and over in the same direction, then gently pull the strings apart so that the disk spins over in the other direction (FIG. 3-4 bottom).

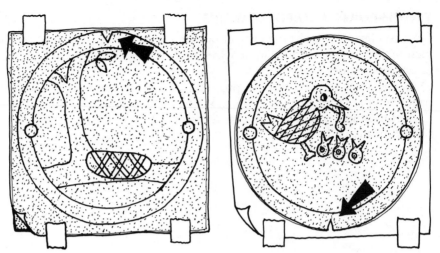

Fig. 3-3 (Left) Trace the circle and the tree design onto a piece of card, and cut it out making sure to cut the "V" notch in the top. Cut holes for string. (Right) Turn the card over so the "V" notch is at the bottom, match up the "V"'s and holes, and trace the birds onto the other side.

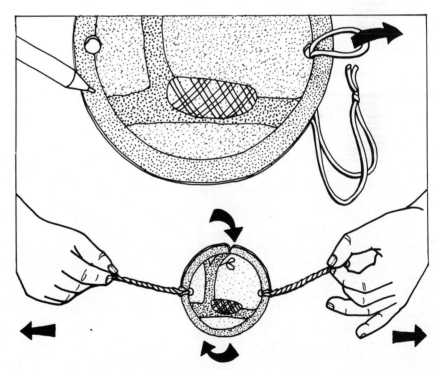

Fig. 3-4 (Top) Color the design in with felt-tip pens and loop string through the holes on each side. (Bottom) To work, wind up by tossing the disk over and over in the same direction. Then pull your hands apart and the disk will flip over in the other direction, the two pictures becoming one, visually.

WATCH-POINT AND FOLLOW-UPS

○ If you like the idea of the project but are not so keen on the birds-in-the-nest picture, how about a mouse and cheese, or a monkey in a cage, or face and eyes, or dogs and bones . . .

○ If you want to speed up the project, you could have the drawings on thin paper and the paper stuck to either side of a flat plastic lid.

○ It is most important that the drawings are the correct way up. Check that the scissor-nick is as described.

Out of the Ark
Ark matchbox animals

In times past, in strict Puritan Christian households, the children were forbidden to play with toys on Sunday. No bicycles, no singing or dancing, no laughing, no running or skipping—the children had to stay in their room and mind their manners. On that one special day of the week, on the "Lord's Day," the children had to spend the "Day of Rest" being absolutely quiet. But it wasn't all bad. Although the children did have to be silent, they were allowed to play with Noah's Ark. Because the Noah story comes from the Bible, the ark and the animals were considered to be religious educational aids and not toys.

If you would like to start a collection of ark animals, then now's your chance. Ask your grandparents if they know a little poem; it goes something like "The animals walked in two by two, the elephant and the kangaroo . . ."

MAKING TIME AND SKILL LEVEL

Although this is really a very simple and basic project, all the various making stages do need to be done with care. With this in mind, I would say that a pair of animals (that is, two cutouts, one stuck each side of the matchbox) can be made by an average 6- to 10-year-old in about 25 to 35 minutes.

Cautions and adult help This project is tricky, but only because the animal shapes need to be carefully drawn out, carefully cut out, and carefully put together. If you are not so good at drawing or scissor work, ask an adult to help you out.

TOOLS AND MATERIALS

☐ Two pieces of thin cardboard, each about 6×3 inches   ☐ A matchbox
☐ A piece of tracing paper   ☐ A pencil and ruler
☐ A tube of quick-set glue   ☐ A pack of colored pencils or crayons.

MEASURE, MARK AND MAKE

I   Have a good look at the project picture (FIG.4-1) and the working pattern (FIG. 4-2), and see how each pair of animals is made up from two cutouts and a matchbox. Note how the cutouts only need to be drawn in and colored on one side.

Continued

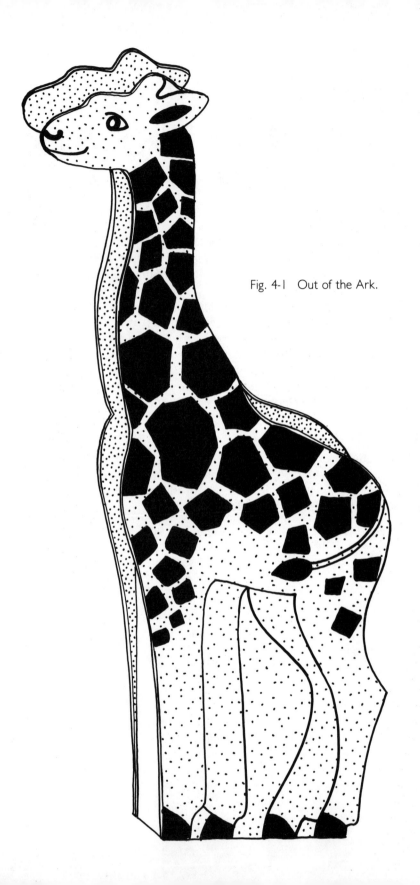

Fig. 4-1 Out of the Ark.

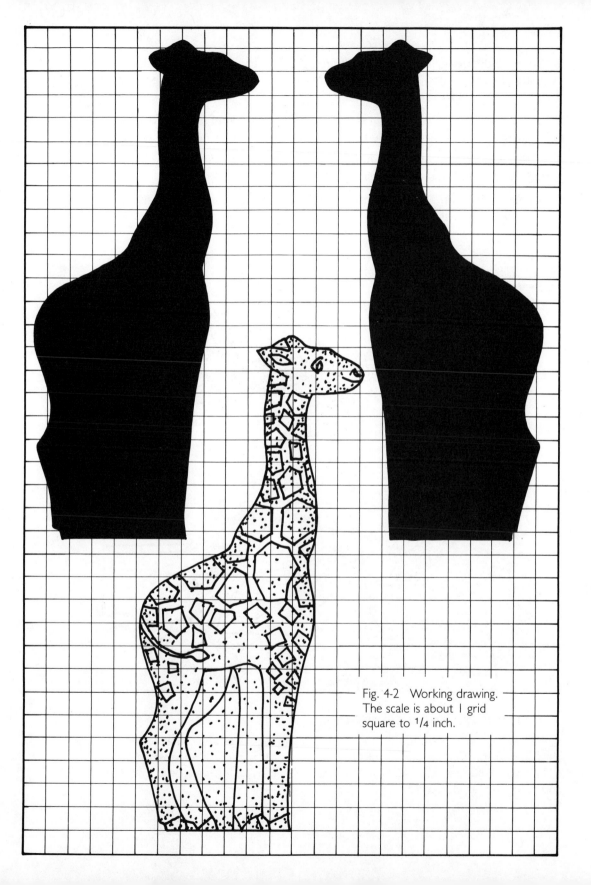

Fig. 4-2 Working drawing.
The scale is about 1 grid
square to 1/4 inch.

2 Trace off the design and then pencil-press-transfer the traced lines through the best face of the card (FIG. 4-3 top). Make sure that you reverse the tracing paper so that you get two mirror-image animals.

3 When you come to cutting out the two giraffes, make sure that the footline or base is cut straight (FIG. 4-3 bottom).

4 When you have cut out both animals, use the colored pencils to color in all the patterns and details that go to make up the design (FIG. 4-4 top).

5 Finally, when you have made two mirror-image giraffes, carefully stick them on each side of the matchbox and set them upright on the worksurface (FIG. 4-4 bottom).

Fig. 4-3 (Top) Trace off the design and pencil-press it through onto the cardboard (make sure you reverse the design when drawing on the second giraffe). (Bottom) Cut out the outline of each giraffe, making sure the feet or base is straight.

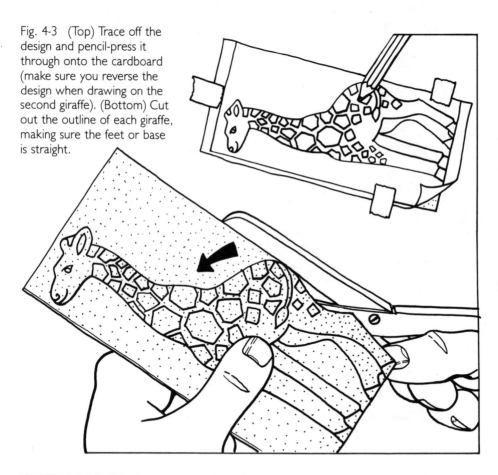

WATCH-POINTS AND FOLLOW-UPS

❍ When you are drawing out and decorating the two giraffes, make sure that they are mirror images. They should be able to look at each other nose-to-nose.
❍ If you decide to make other more-squat animals, like a hippo or a cow, have the matchbox arranged sideways.

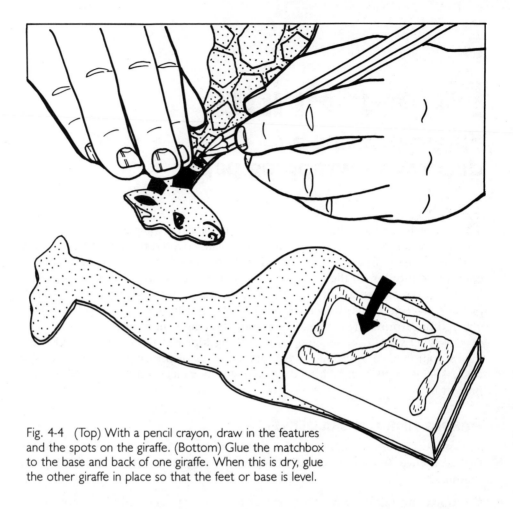

Fig. 4-4 (Top) With a pencil crayon, draw in the features and the spots on the giraffe. (Bottom) Glue the matchbox to the base and back of one giraffe. When this is dry, glue the other giraffe in place so that the feet or base is level.

5
Finger Prints
Finger-printing a decorative wrapping paper

Kids love being messy! Dirty fingerprints all over the wallpaper, sticky jam fingerprints on all the kitchen cupboards, chocolate-covered fingerprints across the furniture, greasy fingerprints on white shirts—children are naturals when it comes to printing with their fingers. Mostly they are moaned and groaned at for leaving marks on just about everything they touch, but not so with this finger-printing project. In this project, the name of the game is to leave big sploshy paint-covered fingerprints. The bigger the prints, the better the results.

Okay all you finger-sticking, mess-making kids out there, don't hold back; this is your chance to go big. If you like the idea of pressing your fingertips in thick, sticky paints and dabbing them across a nice clean surface, then this is the project for you!

MAKING TIME AND SKILL LEVEL

This project is fast and easy; it's the perfect project for young kids. I would say that an average 6- to 12-year-old will have this project finished in about 5 to 10 minutes.

Cautions and adult help This project is very easy. The only help you might need is when you come to cleaning up.

Be warned Finger-printing is fun but only if the working area is carefully defined and you are dressed for the job. Cover the working surface with newspaper, dress yourself from head to foot in old clothes, and warn off pets and parents.

TOOLS AND MATERIALS

☐ A large sheet of plain paper to be printed. Best have it white or pastel-colored.
☐ Acrylic paints ☐ A brush ☐ A plate

MEASURE, MARK AND MAKE

1 Have a look at the project picture (FIG. 5-1) and the pattern page (FIG. 5-2) and see how the paper is folded and printed in two colors. See how the fingerprints are controlled by the folded grid lines.

Continued

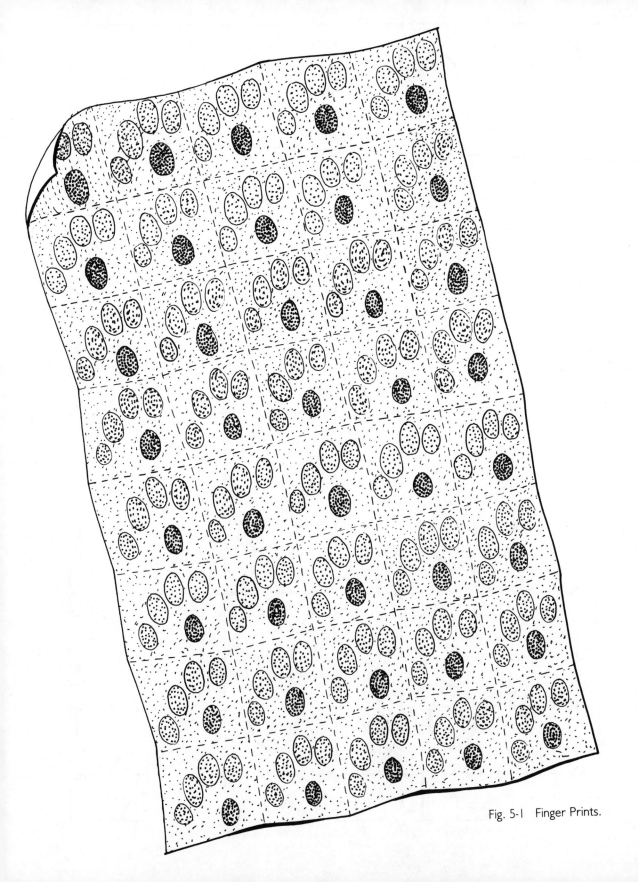

Fig. 5-1 Finger Prints.

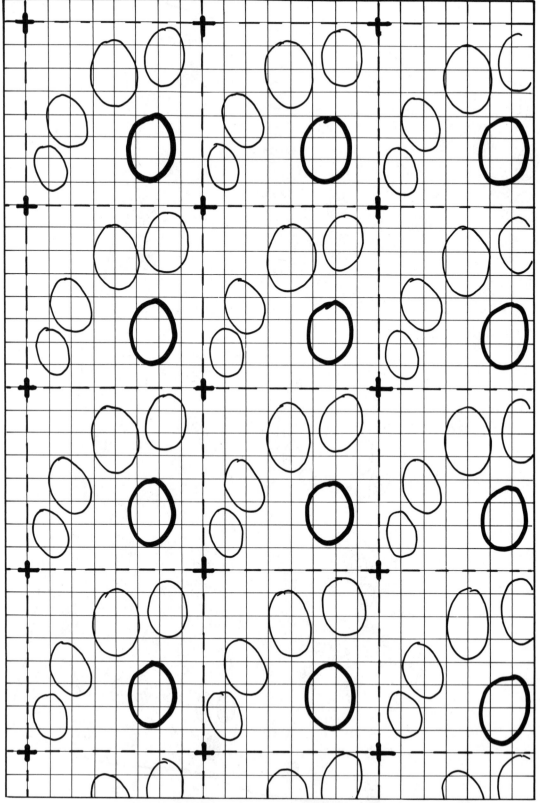

Fig. 5-2 Working drawing. The scale is about 1 grid square to $1/4$ inch.

2   When you have covered the working area with newspaper and set out all the tools and materials, take the paper to be printed and carefully fold it, first one way and then the other, so that it is set out in 2-inch squares (FIG. 5-3 top).

3   Decide on your two colors and the order to be printed, and then brush the first color over the plate to make a thick and even spread (FIG. 5-3 bottom).

4   Hold your four fingers together, press them down onto the paint-covered plate, and then press them firmly onto the first grid square (FIG. 5-4 top).

5   When you have worked backwards and forwards across the paper, making four-finger prints in each of the squares, wash your hands and the paint-covered plate.

6   Finally, brush the second color over the plate, press one finger in the paint, and then work from square to square, printing off the single fingertip color (FIG. 5-4 bottom).

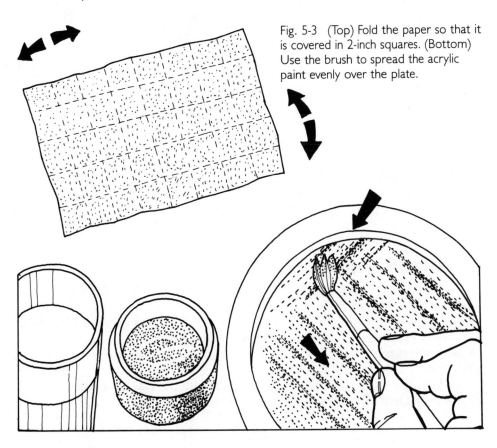

Fig. 5-3   (Top) Fold the paper so that it is covered in 2-inch squares. (Bottom) Use the brush to spread the acrylic paint evenly over the plate.

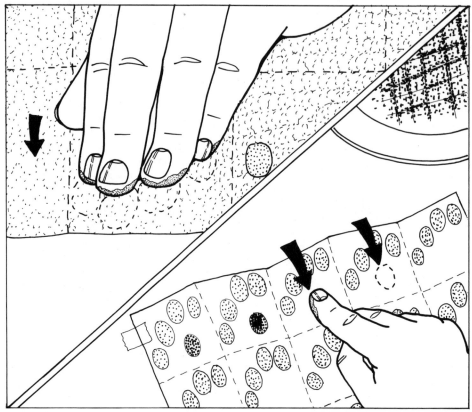

Fig. 5-4 (Top) Holding your fingers together, dip them in the plate of paint and then onto the paper, within one of the squares. (Bottom) Using only one finger and a different color, print under the first print, one in each square.

WATCH-POINTS AND FOLLOW-UPS

○ Make sure that you use water based, nontoxic acrylic paint. *Do not use oil-based enamels or household-gloss colors!*

○ If you like the idea of the project but want to go onto something a bit bigger, how about printing a roll of plain white wall-lining paper?

○ How about printing with your hands and your feet—check this out with an adult first.

○ Acrylic paint dries very quickly, so be ready with the soap and warm water.

○ Some children might need to prepare their hands by using a protective-barrier cream.

Cat's Eyes
A cat's-eyes pocket game

Big cats, cat's cradles, cat's paws, black cats, and weird yellow-green cats eyes gleaming in the night—I think most of us would agree that cats in all their many forms are mysterious and exciting. And much the same might be said for our Cat's-Eye's Pocket Game. Called "cat's eye" because the object of the game is to roll both beads or "eyes" in the sockets, and known as a "pocket game" because its small enough to fit into a small pocket. It's also exciting and good fun.

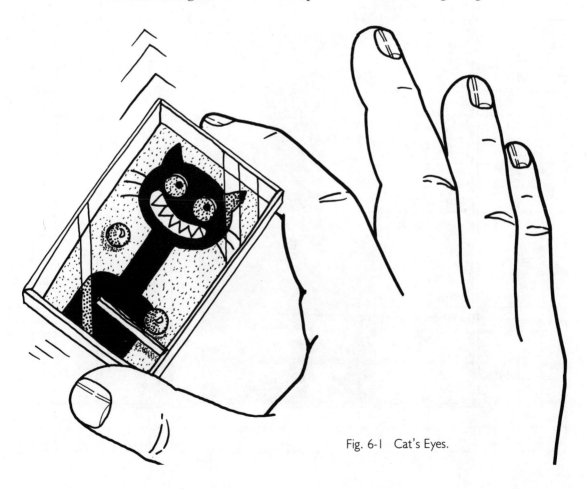

Fig. 6-1 Cat's Eyes.

Fig. 6-2 Working drawings. The scale is about 3 grid squares to ¼ inch.

Fed up with waiting for the morning bus? Bored with television? Got a few minutes to spare between school lessons? This little game is just the thing to wile away all those odd moments. If you like cats, if you like games of skill, and if you like being in the catbird seat, then this is the project for you.

MAKING TIME AND SKILL LEVEL

Easy-to-make, uncomplicated and completely safe. An 8- to 12-year-old could have this project finished in about 20 to 30 minutes.

Cautions and adult help Although this project is safe and relatively easy, it is also small, and its smallness might make it difficult. If you like working with very small things, then you'll have no problem, but if you are a bit clumsy when it comes to working small, then you might just need adult help. Think about it, then ask for adult help if the need arises.

Be warned Small bits of card, small fingers, and small scissors cutting small holes—6- to 7-year-olds might find this project a little bit tricky. Best to take it slow and ask an adult to help you with the extra-special fiddly bits.

TOOLS AND MATERIALS

☐ An empty matchbox
☐ A see-through plastic lid to fit the inside of the box
☐ A sheet of tracing paper   ☐ A pencil and ruler
☐ A pack of colored felt-tip pens   ☐ A paper punch
☐ A couple of small plastic beads to fit the punched holes
☐ A small amount of quick-set glue
☐ A wooden matchstick with tip removed

MEASURE, MARK AND MAKE

1 Have a look at the project picture (FIG. 6-1) and the pattern page (FIG. 6-2) and see how the project is made and put together. Note the way the cat-cutout fits inside the bottom of the box and how the punched eyeholes form little indentations.

2 Slide the top off the matchbox and cut it down so that it fits inside the tray or inner box (FIG. 6-3 top left).

3 Trace off the cat design and pencil-press-transfer the traced lines through to the best face of the tray insert (FIG. 6-3 top middle).

4 Use the hole punch to remove the cat's eyes (FIG. 6-3 top right).

5 Mark out the inside bottom of the tray—the bit behind the eyes—and use the felt-tip pens to color it a greeny yellow (FIG. 6-3 bottom left).

6 Color in the cat with the felt-tip pens. Leave the mouth white (FIG. 6-3 bottom right).

Continued

Fig. 6-3 (Top, left to right) Cut out the top from the outer box, making sure to cut it smaller to fit inside the inner box. Trace the cat design onto the boxtop and use a hole punch to remove the cardboard from the "eyes." (Bottom) Using felt-tip pens to color in the design, color the area inside the box that will be behind the eyes.

7 Stick the cat design down into the base of the bottom of the tray, and glue the matchstick "start-line" in the bottom right-hand corner (FIG. 6-4 top).

8 Finally, when the glue is set, drop the two beads into the box and glue the see-through plastic lid on.

WATCH-POINTS AND FOLLOW-UPS

❍ If you like the idea of the project, but don't like working small, you could use a much larger "family-size" matchbox.

❍ If you want to make a more complicated design, you could have more holes and more beads.

❍ If you can't find a see-through plastic lid to fit the matchbox, you could find a see-through plastic lid and then make a box to fit it.

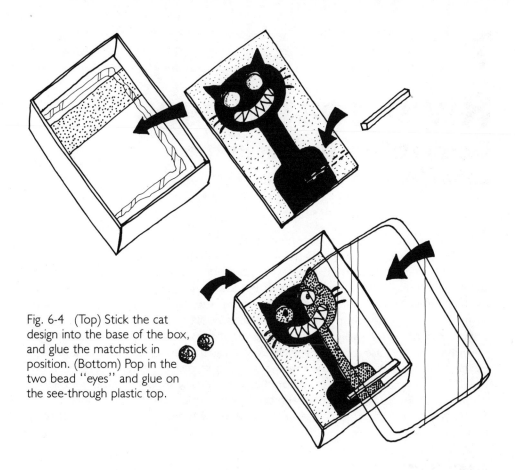

Fig. 6-4 (Top) Stick the cat design into the base of the box, and glue the matchstick in position. (Bottom) Pop in the two bead "eyes" and glue on the see-through plastic top.

7
Riverboat Roses
Decorating a tin can in the canal boat tradition

In England and some parts of America, the term "riverboat roses" is used to describe a certain type of boldly painted and decorated tinware design once used on canal boats. A hundred or so years ago, the poor canal boat families had to live and work on their long narrow boats or barges. In the summer it must have been really good fun—boats slowly chugging along the canals and children running along the canal paths to open lock gates, no schools and only stopping along the way to take on water and coal. But in winter, it must have been cold, damp, and miserable. In any case, the water gypsies or bargemen made the best of a bad job by spending most of their spare time painting and decorating their boats with pictures of flowers. Simple flowers painted on the sides of the barges, flowers on the doors and stools, flowers all over the pots, pans, mugs, and jugs—beautiful!

If you want to brighten up your dull old life, why don't you try a bit of canal boat art?

MAKING TIME AND SKILL LEVEL

Certainly this project is slightly sticky and just a little bit tricky, but for all that, the basic techniques are easy and uncomplicated. Bearing in mind that you need to allow for the paint to dry, an average 8- to 12-year-old should be able to decorate a tin can in a few hours.

Cautions and adult help Best get an adult to help you with this one. Make sure that the empty tin can has a smooth, rounded rim or edge—use a wall-type or an electric can-opener to remove the lid.

Be warned Tin cans and can-openers are dangerous. Ask an adult to pick the can out for you and remove the lid. It must be smooth-rimmed, clean, and dry, with all the paper labels and stickers removed.

TOOLS AND MATERIALS
☐ A clean tin can
☐ Acrylic paint in black, yellow, white, dark green, light green, and red
☐ A couple of broad and fine-point brushes
☐ A pencil and ruler   ☐ A pad of workout paper

MEASURE, MARK AND MAKE

1   Have a good look at the project picture (FIG. 7-1) and the pattern page (FIG. 7-2), and see how the little flowers are painted on a black background. Note the simple brush-worked shapes and the dot-and-dash details.

2   When you have gathered together all your paints and materials, start by giving the tin a generous coat of shiny black paint (FIG. 7-3).

3   While the black paint is drying, practice with the brushes, paint, and workout paper. Let one color dry before you dab on another.

Continued

Fig. 7-1   Riverboat Roses.

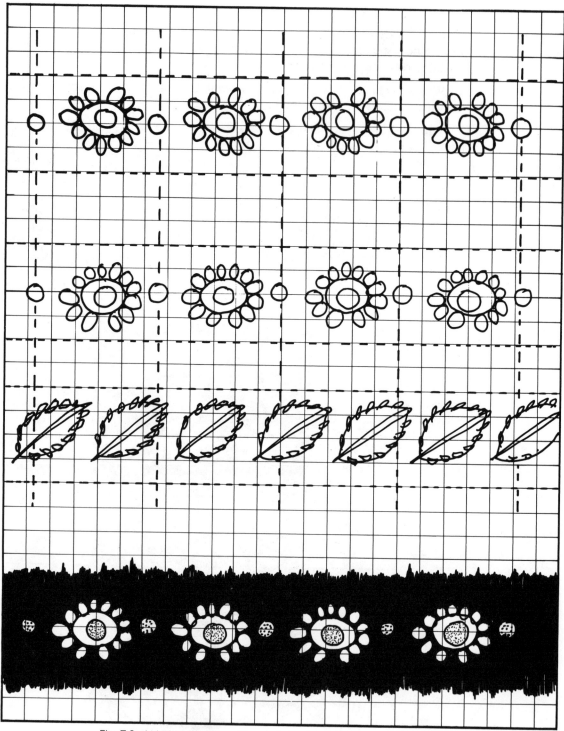

Fig. 7-2 Working drawing. The scale is about I grid square to ¼ inch.

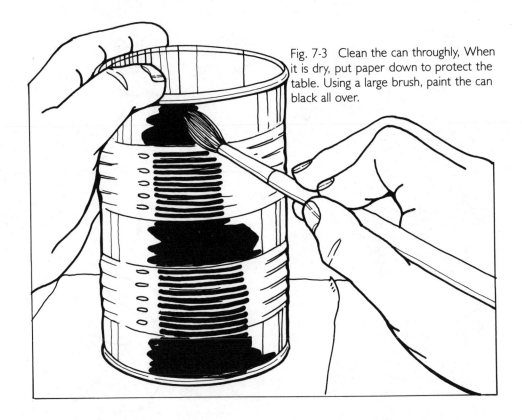

Fig. 7-3 Clean the can throughly, When it is dry, put paper down to protect the table. Using a large brush, paint the can black all over.

4 When you come to painting the flowers, start by loading your brush with bright yellow paint and dabbing in the basic flower form (FIG. 7-4 top left).

5 Next, load a fine-point brush with the white paint, and work around the yellow center, painting in the petals. Work from center-to-side, making one little stroke for each petal (FIG. 7-4 top middle).

6 Finish the flowers off by giving them a dab of red at the centers (FIG. 7-4 top right).

7 When you come to painting the leaves, load a brush with dark green and dab in each of the large, long, slanting shapes with three strokes of the brush (FIG. 7-4 bottom left).

8 When the basic leaf shape is more or less dry, take a fine-point brush and a lighter shade of green, and pick out all the little vein and edge details; use a single brush stroke for the vein and make dots for the spiky edging (FIG. 7-4 bottom right).

9 Finally, work around the flower design, spotting in a dab of green between each of the flowers (FIG. 7-1).

Fig. 7-4 (Top, left to right) Flowers: Paint the yellow center first, then the white petals, starting from the center bottom and radiating around. Then paint the small, red center dot. (Bottom, left to right) Leaves: Paint the dark-green leaf shape and fill in to make it solid. Using a lighter green and a fine brush, paint the center vein and serrated edges of the leaf.

WATCH-POINTS AND FOLLOW-UPS

○ If you have to use oil-based enamel colors, allow extra time for drying

○ If you like the idea of tin painting, you could decorate buckets, coffee pots, enamel mugs, and the like.

○ If you want a really good top-class finish, use matte black rather than shiny black, and finish off by laying on several coats of clear yacht varnish.

Free as a Bird
A glider

Slowly climbing, drifting, and falling on warm currents of air; turning and spinning; and silently swooping across big blue skies—fantastic!

Free as a bird—no noisy engines, just the hissing-whistling-swishing as the glider rushes through the air. Okay, so you haven't flown in a real glider, but not to worry, because now's the time to make your very own miniature stunt glider, and to imagine yourself falling, swooping, and plunging. Our glider is experimental—sometimes it zooms straight and true, other times it loops the loop and nose-dives. Half the pleasure of making and playing with experiments, is the fun you can have trying to figure out the problems. This particular design is so simple that you can broaden the wings, make the tail smaller, or add weight to the nose cone.

Glider flying is a whole heap of fun!

MAKING TIME AND SKILL LEVEL

Although the various making stages aren't, in themselves, especially difficult, it's fair to say that to make a good glider, you do have to be precise and you do have to enjoy careful measuring and cutting.

This is a good project for older children—a 9- to 12-year-old will be able to make a glider in about 1 to 2 hours.

Cautions and adult help If you like measuring, drawing precise straight lines and the like, chances are you won't need any adult help. But, anyway, ask an adult to check out your design before you start cutting, and to show you how best to hold the saw when you come to cutting the cork.

Be warned Glider flying can be dangerous. Stay away from busy roads, greenhouses, windows, powerlines, and crowds of people. When you come to flying the glider, send out warnings to parents, brothers, sisters, and neighbors.

TOOLS AND MATERIALS

- ☐ A 9-x-6-inch sheet of cardboard—best if it's stiff and white
- ☐ A pencil and ruler   ☐ A 1/4-inch-diameter dowel about 10 inches long
- ☐ A couple of sheets of sandpaper   ☐ A straight-sided wine bottle cork
- ☐ A small saw   ☐ A tube of balsa glue/cement   ☐ A pair of scissors
- ☐ A selection of acrylic paints   ☐ A couple of brushes
- ☐ A blob of Blu Tack, or a "sticking-posters-on-the-wall-type" low-tack plastic putty.

Fig. 8-1   Free as a Bird.

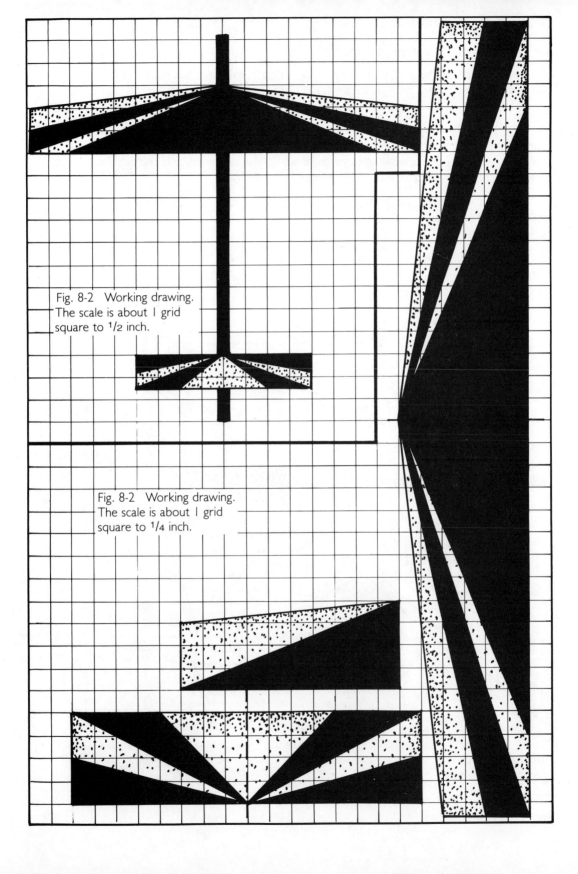

Fig. 8-2   Working drawing. The scale is about 1 grid square to 1/2 inch.

Fig. 8-2   Working drawing. The scale is about 1 grid square to 1/4 inch.

MEASURE, MARK AND MAKE

1   Have a look at the project picture (FIG. 8-1) and the working drawings (FIG. 8-2), and see how the 1/4-inch-diameter dowel runs from nose to tail. Note how the round dowel section has been sliced and flattened to take the wings.

2   When you have a good understanding of how the project is made and put together, take the pencil, ruler, and cardboard, and draw and trace out the three cardboard shapes or profiles: the large front wing, the tail wing, and the tail. Best make the tail from slightly thicker cardboard (FIG. 8-3 top).

3   Check and double-check that all is correct, then use the pencil and ruler to draw in the center lines and to transfer all the patterns through to the cardboard (FIG. 8-3 top left).

4   Use the scissors to cut out the three cardboard forms. Aim for crisp straight lines.

Continued

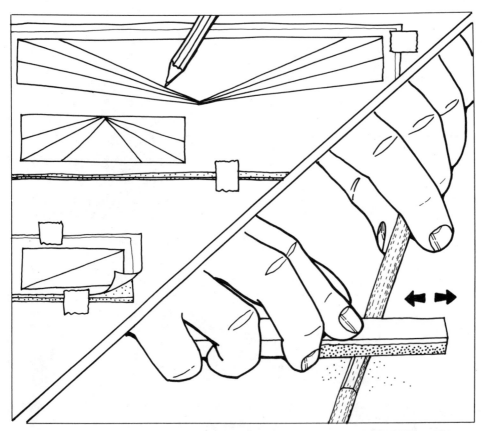

Fig. 8-3   (Top Left) Pencil-press-transfer the design onto the cardboard. Note: The tail is cut from thicker cardboard. (Bottom Right) Sand the two areas on the stick (or dowel) so that it is ready to receive the wings and the tail.

5 Take the 10-inch-long dowel and label one end "nose" and the other end "tail". Then measure and mark in the position of the two wings—the front wing is set 1½ inches back from the nose, and the small rear wing is set ½ inch along from the tail.

6 When you have marked in the position of the two wings, support the sandpaper with a flat scrap of wood. Rub away the top side of the dowel until the wing areas or wing beds are flat and smooth (FIG. 8-3 bottom).

7 Use the quick-set balsa glue/cement to fit-and-fix the wings and tail to the dowel fuselage. Build the glue up until the joints are reinforced (FIG. 8-4 top).

8 Make a pencil-size hole in one end of the cardboard, spike the nose end of the dowel in the hole, and have a trial flight.

9 Cut slices off the cork and add pieces of Blu Tack-type putty until the glider flies level, straight, and fast (FIG. 8-4 bottom).

Continued

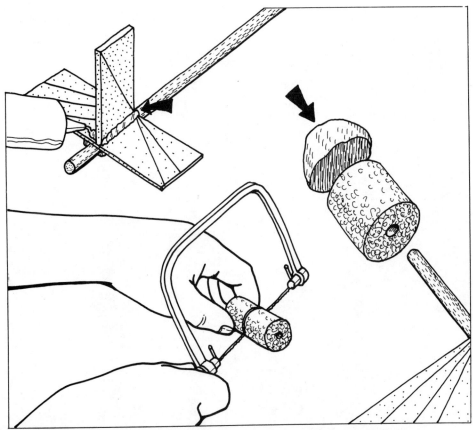

Fig. 8-4 (Top Left) Glue the tail in place, running extra glue along the joints to reinforce them. (Bottom Left) Saw the cork to the right size. (Bottom Right) Glue the cork onto the stick/dowel, and fashion the putty weight on the end.

10 Finally, glue the cork on the dowel, shape the putty nose cone (FIG. 8-4 right), and use the acrylic paint to block in the areas of color that go to make up the design.

WATCH-POINTS AND FOLLOW-UPS

○ If you decide to use a much larger-size dowel, note that you will also need to make the dowel longer and the wings larger. Have several experimental tryouts with scrap wood and cardboard before you cut into your best materials.

○ When you come to sanding down the two wing beds, make sure that they are both on the topside of the dowel.

○ Give the glue plenty of time to set.

○ When you come to flying the glider, make sure that you are well away from busy roads, powerlines, windows, and pets.

Caribbean Carnival
A set of carnival drums

Sunshine, tropical islands, blue seas, palm trees, sweet potatoes, yams, warm brown colors, golden sands, steel pan drums, music, and carnivals—fantastic! So where is this paradise? Well, if you haven't guessed already, it's Jamaica, Puerto Rico, Cuba, Trinidad, and all the other beautiful islands that make up the Caribbean. When I think of the Caribbean, I think mostly about carnivals, dancing, and music. And when I think of the music, I think about steel drum bands and the rhythmic, pulsing beat of drums and maracas.

Okay, so maybe you have never been to the Caribbean, and perhaps you don't know too much about the people and the traditions, but this is not to say that you can't make a set of Caribbean-type drums and let rip with the music. Looking forward to a school dance? A friend's party? A fancy dress party? Or even a carnival procession? Well, how about making yourself a set of drums! They look good, they sound good, and they are great fun to make!

MAKING TIME AND SKILL LEVEL

An easy-to-make, relatively safe project. An average 6- to 12-year-old should be able to put the drums together in about 30 to 90 minutes.

Cautions and adult help Cutting the plastic containers down to size and putting together is easy enough, but the initial marking out is just a little bit tricky. You might need some adult help right at the start of the project.

Be warned Drums are wonderful—the rhythmic pulsing, the steady beat, beat, beat—but think about it, will your parents and grandparents enjoy the noise? Ask around and see if drums are a good idea.

TOOLS AND MATERIALS

- ☐ Six plastic food containers, we have used plain soft white plastic dried milk powder containers. They are about 7 inches high and 3½ inches in diameter.
- ☐ A strong cardboard box to take the six containers.
- ☐ A roll of masking tape ☐ A pencil and felt-tip pen
- ☐ A pair of scissors ☐ A large long bodkin needle
- ☐ A reel of strong nylon fishing line
- ☐ A good selection of acrylic paints
- ☐ A couple of paintbrushes—one broad and the other fine-point.
- ☐ Two corks ☐ Two lollipop sticks

MEASURE, MARK AND MAKE

I Have a look at the project picture (FIG. 9-1) and the working drawing (FIG. 9-2) and see how the project is made up from the six plastic food drums and a cardboard box. Note how the containers have been trimmed so that they range in height from the 7-inch-high uncut container, through to one that is about 1 to 2 inches high.

Continued

Fig. 9-1 Carribbean Drums.

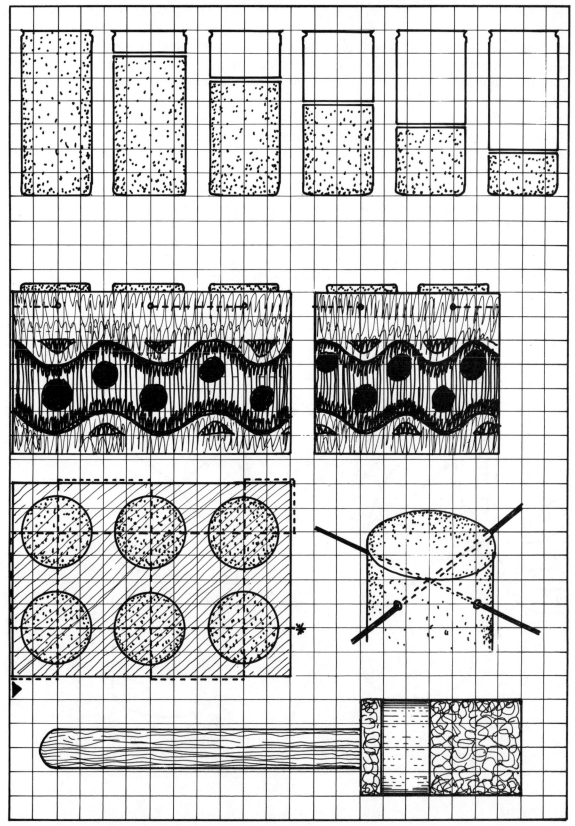

Fig. 9-2 Working drawing. The scale is about 1 grid square to 1 inch. (Mallet not to scale.)

2   When you know how the project goes together, take the ruler and the felt-tip pen and mark out the six containers (FIG. 9-3 left). Depending on the size of your containers, you might have the smallest one 2 inches high, the next one 3 inches high, and so on.

3   Bearing in mind that the waste is always going to occur at the rim end of the container, take the scissors and trim the containers to size. Cut in from the rim, and gradually snip around and around until you are working on the cutting line (FIG. 9-3 top right).

4   With the drums cut to size, turn them over so that they are bottom-side-up and use the bodkin to make the four string holes (FIG. 9-3 bottom right).

5   Trim the cardboard box down to size and cover the cut edge with strips of masking tape.

6   Set the six containers in a stepped sequence in the cardboard box.

Continued

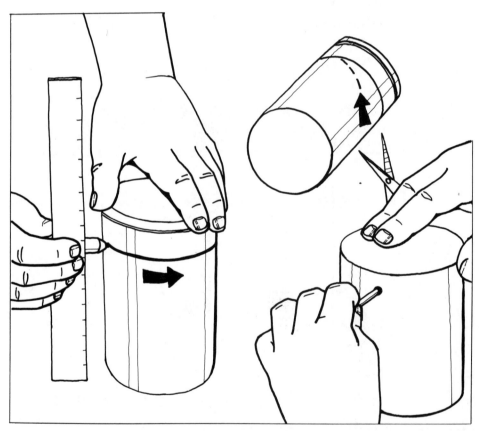

Fig. 9-3   (Left) Use a ruler and felt-tip pen to mark off the various heights on the containers. (Top Right) Cutting the containers is not difficult if you spiral into the cutting line gradually with sharp-pointed scissors. (Bottom Right) Pierce the four holes in each container.

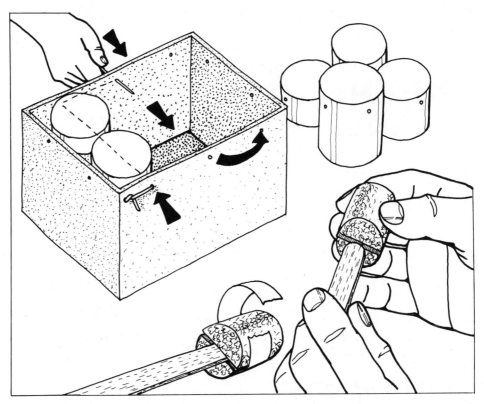

Fig. 9-4 (Top Left) Using a large bodkin, thread the containers onto the fishing twine, in position in the box. (Bottom) Cut a slot in the corks. Glue in the sticks and bind with tape.

7 Thread the bodkin up with the nylon fishing twine. Run the twine from the start point on the box, backwards and forwards, from box-side to box-side and through the containers, until all six drums are held in space base-side up and level with the top of the cardboard box (FIG. 9-4 top left).

8 With each drum being held taut by a side-to-side and back-to-front X, knot the twine off.

9 When you come to making the two drumsticks, slice the two corks down with the saw-tooth knife, set the lollipop sticks in the slots, and strap the cork up with the masking tape (FIG. 9-4 bottom right).

10 Finally, use the brushes and the acrylic paint to decorate the box and the drum sticks with the patterns of your choice.

WATCH-POINTS AND FOLLOW-UPS

○ You will have to adjust all the measurements, widths, and heights to fit the size of your plastic food containers.
○ Bearing in mind that the longest drum makes the deepest noise, set the drums out in the box in a stepped order. You could number them.

10

Hoppity Hare
A matchbox toy

Rabbits, hares, Bugs Bunny, cottontails, hoppities, thumpers, and bunny rabbits—they are all beautiful. Okay, so they do, from time to time, raid our gardens and eat our vegetables, and they do annoy farmers by eating acres and acres of grass, but for all that, they are wonderful creatures. With their loppy-long ears, twitchy noses and whiskers, soft smooth coats, large black-button eyes, and powder-puff tails, I think that our world is all the better for having them around.

Our Hoppity Hare is a great-fun critter. Stand him up on the table and quickly open and close the matchbox. Hoppity will look to be jumping, thumping, munching, and generally having a grand old time. If you want to make a little toy for a friend, or you just want to have fun watching hoppity do his act, then I've got a feeling that this is the project for you.

MAKING TIME AND SKILL LEVEL

This is one of those speedy, snip-clip-and-glue projects that you can have all wrapped up and made in less time than it takes to sneeze. Well . . . almost!

Needing not much more than a matchbox, a scrap of paper, a pair of scissors, and a couple of tabs of sticky tape, a 7- to 10-year-old can make this project in about 10 to 15 minutes.

Cautions and adult help If you can handle a pair of scissors, then no problem, you can manage this project on your own. It's easy and it's fun. If you make a bit of a mess when you come to drawing in Hoppity's nose or whiskers, no sweat, you just take another scrap of card and start over again.

TOOLS AND MATERIALS

☐ A small piece of thin cardboard about 6 × 4 inches. Best if its a soft pastel color on both sides
☐ A scrap of tracing paper   ☐ An empty matchbox   ☐ A pencil and ruler
☐ A pair of scissors   ☐ A few inches of double-sided sticky tape

MEASURE, MARK AND MAKE

I Have a look at the project picture (FIG. 10-1) and the pattern page (FIG. 10-2), and see how the little hoppity toy is no more than a hare/rabbit cutout and a

Continued

Fig. 10-1 Hoppity Hare.

matchbox. See how the cutout is fixed to the box so that the opening and closing action sets the hare thumping and jumping.

2 Take a tracing from the master design and pencil-press-transfer the traced lines through to the piece of thin cardboard (FIG. 10-3 top).

3 When you have a clear outline drawn on the card, first clear away the main areas of waste, and then cut out the fine details (FIG. 10-3 bottom). Don't forget to leave the long base strip.

Continued

Hoppity Hare   47

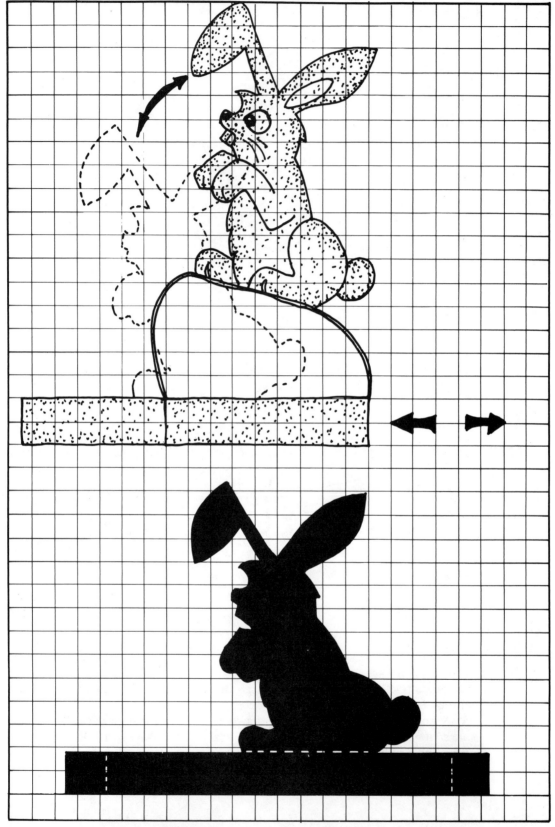

Fig. 10-2 Working drawing. The scale is about 1 grid square to ¹/₄ inch.

Fig. 10-3 (Top Left) Take a tracing of the design and pencil-press-transfer the design to the piece of cardboard. (Bottom) Cut away the waste and cut into the detailed areas, making sure to leave the lines of the design.

4 Use a felt-tip pen to draw in all the little details that make up the design, the teeth, the eyes, the whiskers, and the like. Draw on both sides of the card (FIG. 10-4 top left).

5 Finally, fold the card strip up so that it is at right angles to the hare, and use the sticky tape to fit-and-fix the ends of the strip to the opened-out matchbox (FIG. 10-4 bottom).

WATCH-POINTS AND FOLLOW-UPS

○ If you want to use a large family-size matchbox, then you will need to change the length of the strip/cutout to fit your chosen box.
○ If you like the idea of the project, but are not so keen on the hare/rabbit, then why not draw in another animal? How about, a monkey, a cat, a dog, a mouse, a bug, a chipmonk, or a....?
○ If you don't much like drawing, you could use a magazine cutout or maybe even a family photograph.

Fig. 10-4 (Top Left) Use a pen to line in the design on both sides of the hare, color the eye and teeth white. (Bottom Right) Fold the hare up along the fold line, and the flaps down along the fold line. Use double-sided tape to attach the flaps to the matchbox.

Bobbing Bug
A ceiling decoration

Do you like bugs? No, I don't mean those horrible germs or defects in computer programs or those nasty small microphones used by spys, I mean those delightful little insects that at night fly, buzz, and whirr in through the bedroom window. Shiny wings, lots of little legs, hairy antenna and big black eyes—most children love them. Certainly wasps, earwings, wood termites and cockroaches aren't so wonderful, but beetles, cicadas and crickets are really beautiful.

Maybe your mom and dad have put a stop to your bug collection. Not to worry, our giant concertina or accordian-style Bobbing Bug is so friendly that even your parents will like him. Hang him from the ceiling on a piece of thin elastic and then stand back and watch him bob up and down. He's really great. What shall we call him, how about Bert, Betty, Barrie, or . . . ??

MAKING TIME AND SKILL LEVEL

Although this project is a little bit finger-twisting, I would say that if you really get down to work, you could get your bug made in about 20 minutes. A good clean simple-to-make project—you could, without fuss and bother, easily make it on the kitchen table.

Cautions and adult help If you don't know how to use a pair of scissors and a stapler, then now is the time to learn. If you are a beginner, best use a pair of round-point scissors and a small mini-pocket stapler. Ask your parents for help.

TOOLS AND MATERIALS

- ☐ A sheet of tracing paper
- ☐ A piece of colored paper or thin cardboard about 6×9 inches. Best if it's plain and brightly colored on both sides.
- ☐ A good supply of thin colored paper at about 5×5 inches. You need at least 20 pieces.
- ☐ A pencil and ruler   ☐ A pair of scissors   ☐ A small pocket stapler
- ☐ A length of thin elastic   ☐ A tube of clear quick-set glue

MEASURE, MARK AND CUT

1 Have a good look at the project picture (FIG. 11-1) and the pattern page (FIG. 11-2), and see how the bug is made up from layers of colored paper. See how, by

Continued

Fig. 11-1 Bobbing Bug.

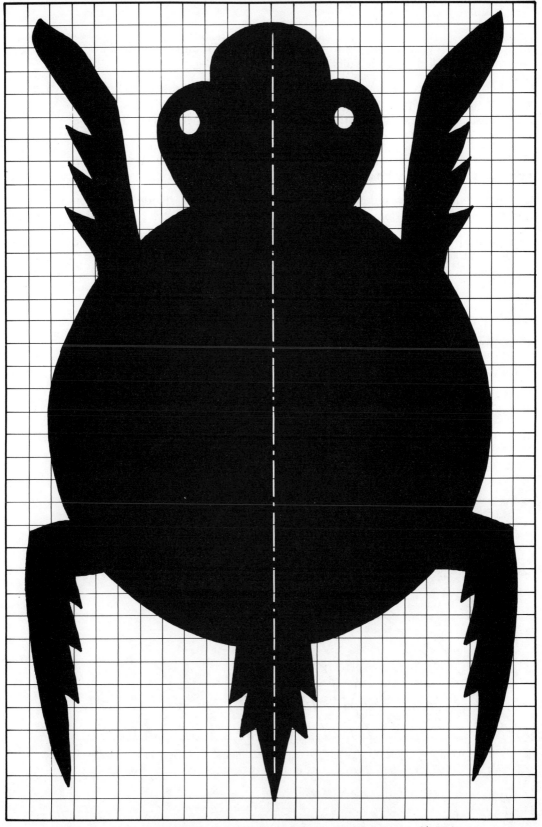

Fig. 11-2 Working drawing. The scale is about 1 grid square to ¹/4 inch.

gluing and stapling, it is possible to give the bug a fat, round concertina body; have a careful look at how the pairs of papers or "pages" are stapled.

2 When you have worked out how the separate circles of paper need to be fixed, trace off the two shapes: the large bug and the 5-inch-diameter circle. Pencil-press-transfer the traced outlines through to the colored paper. You need one bug shape and 20 circles (FIG. 11-3 top).

3 Use the scissors to cut out the drawn shapes, the bug, and the 20 circles, and then fold each of the circles and the bug into half (FIG. 11-3 bottom).

4 Making sure that the different colors are well spread about, divide the 20 colored circles up into two piles of 10.

5 Arrange the circles so that all the centerlines are aligned, and then staple through the fold lines so that each stack of ten circles is fixed together with at least two staples.

Continued

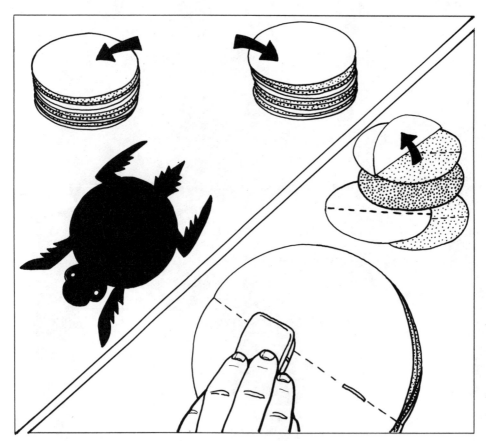

Fig. 11-3 (Top) Make two piles of 10 each and cut out one bug shape. (Bottom) Crease each circle of paper in half and staple them in units of 10 in two places on the crease.

6 Smear a little glue on both sides of the main bug cutout and, making sure that all the centerline folds are sitting directly one on top of another, make a circles-bug-and-circles sandwich.

7 When the glue is dry, set the bug sandwich flat-down on the worksurface. Then starting with the top-most pair of "pages," work around the bug, stapling neighboring pairs of circles together. Have each pair of "pages" fixed with a single staple set on the outermost edge (FIG. 11-4 top).

8 When you have worked right round the bug, fixing pairs of half-circles together with single staples at top-center, gently ease the paired "pages" apart and carefully link up neighboring pairs so that they are fixed with two staples (FIG. 11-4 bottom).

9 Finally, when you have worked right around the bug with neighboring pages 1 and 2 fixed with one staple, 2 and 3 with two staples, 3 and 4 with one staple, and so on, give the bug a couple of punched eye holes, hang him up by his thin piece of elastic and then stand back and watch him bob and boiingggggggg!

Fig. 11-4 (Top Left) Staple the half circles of colored paper in pairs at the center edge. (Bottom Right) Separate the pairs, then regroup them and staple them in two places on the edge.

WATCH-POINTS AND FOLLOW-UPS

○ When you are choosing your materials, best go for thin bright-colored paper for the circles and a slightly thicker paper for the bug's body.

○ If you are very clever with your fingers, you could use instant quick-set glue rather than staples. It would make for a better bug.

○ If you aren't quite sure how the pages need to be fixed, have a trial put-together with paper clips.

○ If you are using very thin brightly colored tissue papers, be careful that the glue doesn't make the colors run.

Rattling Reptile
A Central American toy

There is in Central America a tradition of making the most beautiful art and crafts objects. The Indians, men, women, and children, make baskets, pottery, banners, beaded belts, wood carvings, tinware, and small wooden toys. With a few simple tools, a saw and a knife, and with salvaged crate-wood collected from the markets, they make really exciting toys—everything from wriggling snakes, clicking fish, and fluttering birds, to dolls, drums, and little rattling reptile geckoes or lizards.

Bearing in mind that many of the toys in Central America are made by children, why don't you see if you can make a little working rattling reptile—a small piece of thin wood, 10 minutes or so with a coping saw, a few inches of knotted cord, and five minutes spent with a brush and a splash or two of colored paint, and almost before you can wink and blink, you will have a really exciting folk toy. It's easy and its fun!

MAKING TIME AND SKILL LEVEL

No problem with this project, as long as you know how to use a coping saw and a hand drill. Older children, say 9- to 12-year-olds, could have this toy made and working in about 30 to 40 minutes.

Cautions and adult help   Coping saws and small hand drills are safe enough, as long as you take it slowly and one step at a time, and as long as you are sensible. The very worst you can do is to graze your fingers with the saw or nip yourself in the jaws of the drill chuck. In any case, if you are at all unsure, ask an adult for help.

Be warned   By hand drill, I mean a small, easy-to-use, hand-operated drill—*not an electric drill.*

TOOLS AND MATERIALS

☐ A small amount of thin multicore plywood   ☐ A pencil and ruler
☐ A sheet of tracing paper   ☐ A coping saw
☐ The use of a workbench and a vice   ☐ A small hand-operated drill
☐ A $1/8$-inch-diameter bit to fit the drill   ☐ A ball of string
☐ A selection of acrylic paints   ☐ A couple of small brushes
☐ A pair of pliers and a small amount of thin wire
☐ A sheet of medium-fine sandpaper

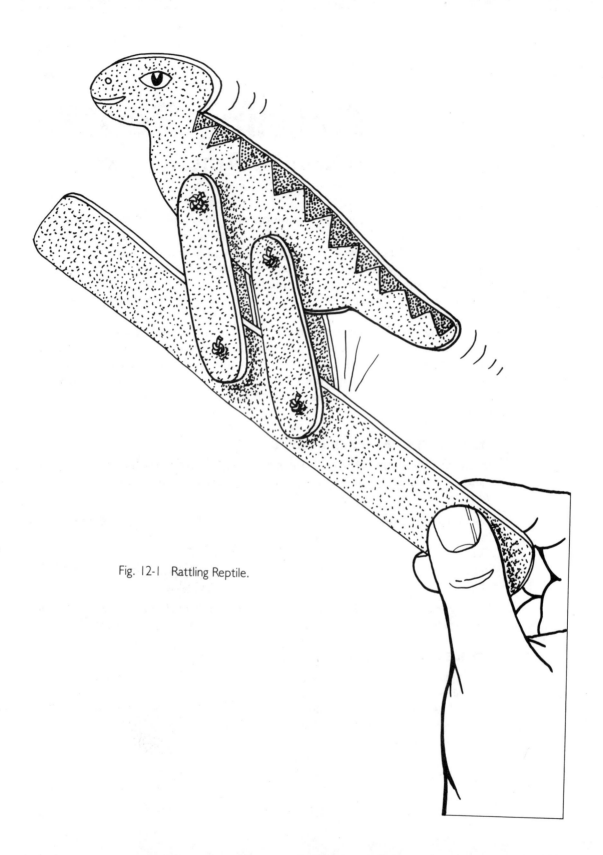

Fig. 12-1   Rattling Reptile.

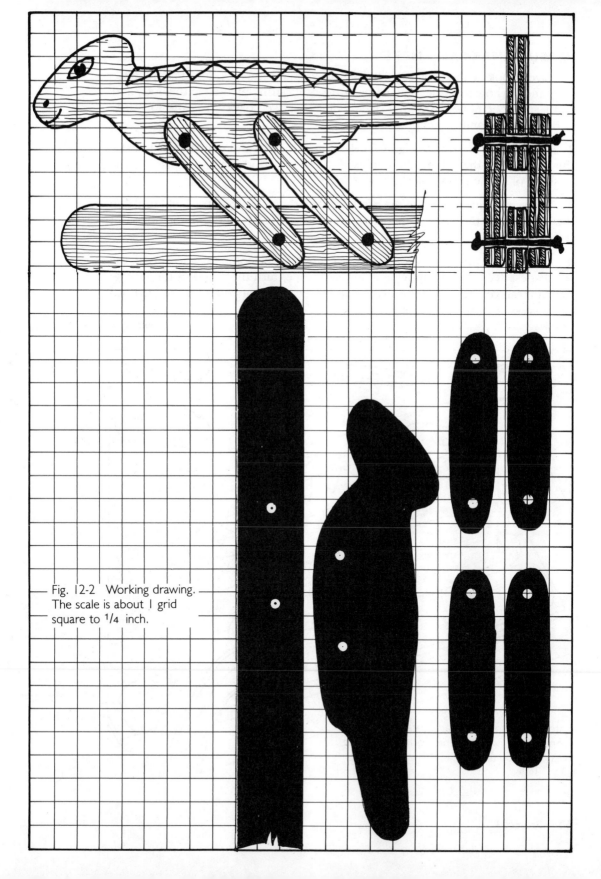

Fig. 12-2 Working drawing. The scale is about 1 grid square to 1/4 inch.

MEASURE, MARK AND MAKE

1 Have a look at the project picture (FIG. 12-1) and the working drawing (FIG. 12-2), and see how the little reptile's legs are loosely string-pivoted to the body and to the stick. See how; in use, the stick is quickly jerked backwards and forwards so that the little animal jumps and clicks.

2 Trace off all the parts that go to make up the project and pencil-press-transfer the traced lines through to the best face of the plywood. Carefully mark in the position of all the pivot holes (FIG. 12-3 top).

3 When you have marked in the position of all the holes, take the hand drill and the 1/8-inch drill bit, support the wood on a piece of scrap, and drill the holes out (FIG. 12-3).

4 Support the drilled plywood in the vice, and use the coping saw to cut out the six shapes. Keep the saw moving at a steady pace, turn the wood in the vice so that you can get around all the shapes, and make sure that you keep the blade on the waste-side of the drawn line (FIG. 12-4).

Continued

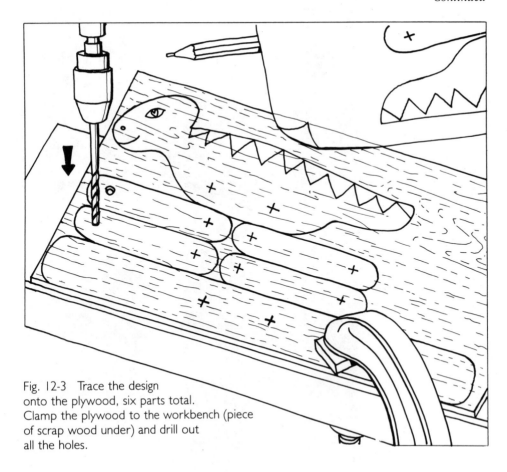

Fig. 12-3   Trace the design
onto the plywood, six parts total.
Clamp the plywood to the workbench (piece
of scrap wood under) and drill out
all the holes.

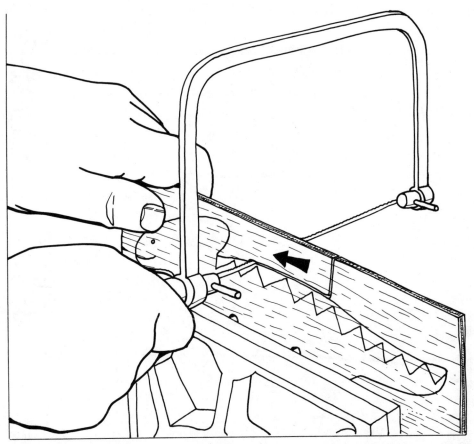

Fig. 12-4 Put the drilled plywood into the vice. With a coping saw travel around the six shapes, turning the blade to best advantage and altering the portion of the ply in the vice to "get around" all the shapes. Cut on the outside of the drawn line.

5 When you have drilled and cut out the six shapes, the body, the four legs, and the base stick, take the sandpaper and rub all the cut edges down to a smooth, slightly rounded finish.

6 Before you start painting the wooden cutouts, make a knotted drying line and a good number of small wire "S" hooks (FIG. 12-5 top).

7 Lay on a generous ground or base coat, paint in the decorative details, and then hang the parts up to dry (FIG. 12-5 top).

8 When the paint is dry, take the legs-body-legs sandwich, make sure that the holes are well aligned, and then make and knot the little cord pivots. Use large double knots and make sure that the pivot-fit is loose and easy (FIG. 12-5 bottom).

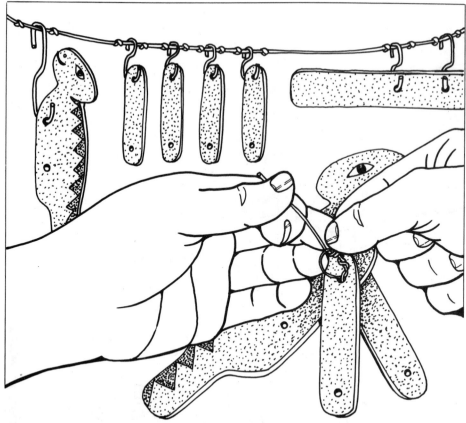

Fig. 12-5 (Top) Make a line with small knots at regular intervals on which to hang the painted pieces up to dry. (Bottom) Assembling the reptile: Use large knots, tied again and again to form the joints. They must be loose enough to allow the legs to move easily.

WATCH-POINTS AND FOLLOW-UPS

○ If you have never used a coping saw before, be ready with a pack of spare blades.

○ When you are drilling out the holes, use a scrap of wood for a backing board—this way you won't splinter the back of the plywood or drill holes in the bench.

○ Don't try to saw too fast; take it at a slow, steady, even pace. Try to make sure that the saw blade passes through the wood at a good square angle.

○ Let the top coat dry out before you paint in the details.

○ If your knots are a bit of a mess, make sure that they stay put by dabbing them with a spot of clear quick-set glue.

13

Trembling Tarantula
A traditional bristle dancing toy

Bristle dolls are really good fun! Known variously over the centuries as Chinese dancers, minuet dolls, harpsicord dancers, piano dolls, gramaphone dancers, and even—much closer to our own time—as Microphone Sammies, bristle dolls are little figures that look to be dancing and moving when they are placed on top of a vibrating surface.

Our Trembling Tarantula is a really terrific, tail-wagging, talented, tango-dancing smooth-mover. Place him on top of, say, the radio, and when the radio is switched on, he will look as if he is dancing. The louder the radio, the more he will dance. Place him on a little plate or tray, place the tray on top of the TV, and then you will be able to watch him dance the night away. It could be really good fun, you could make whole families. Just think on it, you could have tribes of tarantulas all trembling on top of the TV.

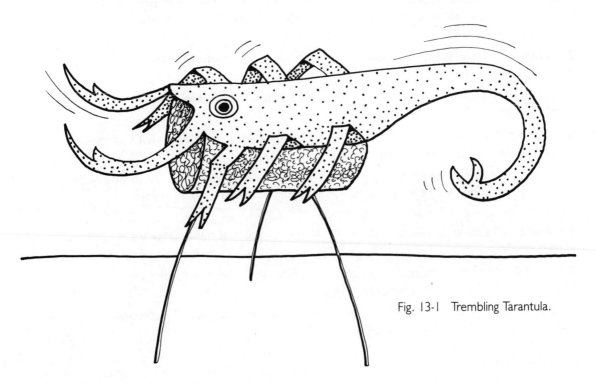

Fig. 13-1 Trembling Tarantula.

MAKING TIME AND SKILL LEVEL

Would you believe, that our trembling terror can be made in about 10 to 15 minutes? You don't need to be a junior high school genius, all you need is a cork, a scrap of paper, and three stiff bristles cut from a yard broom. The rest is easy. Ask your parents about the broom bristles!

Cautions and adult help   You do need to use a needle or spike to make the holes in the cork, so best ask you parents for help at the hole-making stage. When you are making the holes, watch out that the cork doesn't split apart. Be sure to work on a board.

TOOLS AND MATERIALS

☐ A wine cork about 2 inches long and 1 inch in diameter
☐ Three stiff bristles from a yard broom—they can be natural or made of plastic
☐ A piece of thin colored paper about 6×3 inches.
☐ A sheet of tracing paper   ☐ A pencil and ruler
☐ A hole-making tool—you could use a darning needle or a spiked fork from the kitchen. *Ask your parents!*
☐ A pair of scissors   ☐ A tube of clear quick-set glue

MEASURE, MARK AND MAKE

I Have a look at the project picture (FIG. 13-1) and the pattern page (FIG. 13-2), and see how the tarantula is easily made from the cork and the three stiff bristles. See how the bristles are push-fixed in one side of the cork, while the tarantula cutout is stuck to the other.

2 When you have gathered together all you tools and materials, clear the worksurface and carefully trace off the tarantula design.

3 Pencil-press-transfer the tarantula outline through to the best face of the sheet of colored paper (FIG. 13-3 top left).

4 Use the scissors to cut out the tarantula—go easy and be extra careful that you don't snip off his legs (FIG. 13-3 top right).

5 When your parents or perhaps an older brother or sister has spiked the three holes in the "underside" of the cork, push-fit the three bristles into the holes (FIG. 13-3 bottom).

6 Trim bristles to length so that the cork is able to stand upright like a three-legged stool.

7 Carefully bend the tarantula's legs up and then down, so as to give him knee-like joints (FIG. 13-4 top). Pencil in the eyes.

8 Finally, squeeze a little glue over the "topside" of the three-legged cork, and press the tarantula cutout into position.

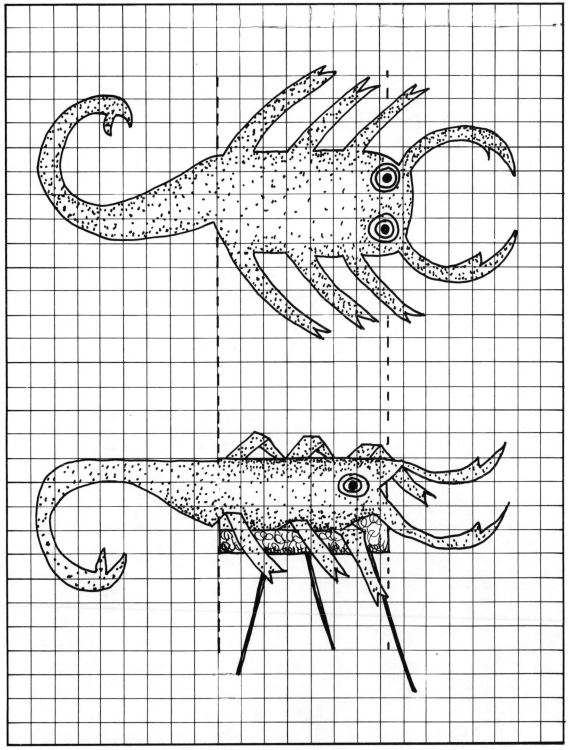

Fig. 13-2 Working drawing. The scale is about I grid square to ¹⁄4 inch.

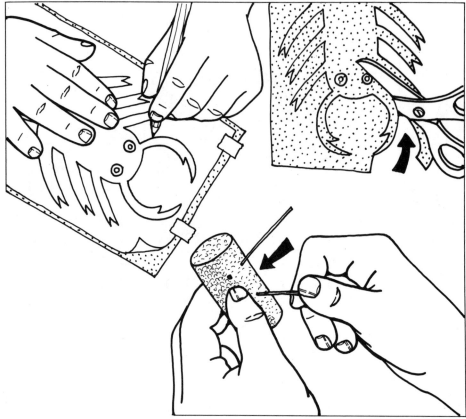

Fig. 13-3 (Top Left) Trace the tarantula design through onto a small piece of colored cardboard. (Top Right) Cut out the design. (Bottom) Push the bristles into the holes on the "underside" of the cork.

WATCH-POINTS AND FOLLOW-UPS

○ A sticky cork all covered in wine or somesuch is not a good idea! Make sure that the cork is clean and dry.

○ If you like the idea of the project but don't much like the idea of the tarantula, how about making say a dog or cat or mouse or spider or . . . .

○ The colored paper needs to thin, but not so thin that it bends under its own weight; the tarantulas legs shouldn't sag.

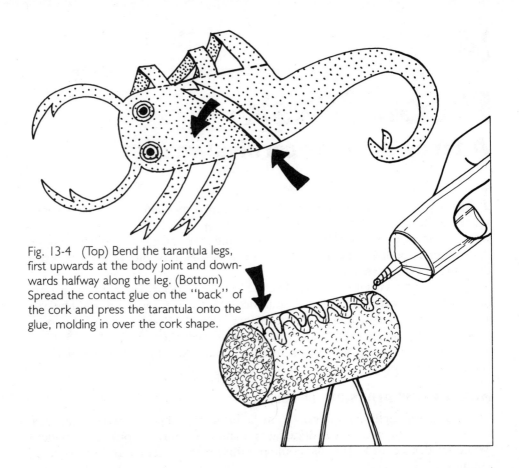

Fig. 13-4 (Top) Bend the tarantula legs, first upwards at the body joint and downwards halfway along the leg. (Bottom) Spread the contact glue on the "back" of the cork and press the tarantula onto the glue, molding in over the cork shape.

14

Moon Mask
A fancy dress or carnival mask

I wish I were more handsome . . . I wish I were a monster . . . I wish I were a space traveler . . . I wish I could really scare people at Halloween time, I wish I were . . . bigger, better, and badder! At some time or other, most of us have wished to be different people. Of course we don't really want to be different, it's just that the same old face gets to be a bit boring.

Just imagine what it would feel like to have a huge beard, or a long nose, or to be wearing a crown. Wouldn't it be fantastic if for just a moment we could be, say, a monster, or a space man, or the Lone Ranger, or Robin Hood, or a beautiful princess? Okay, so you are stuck with your face, but what about a mask?

Masks are amazing—our moon mask will make you feel taller, grander, and altogether more powerful. It's great fun!

MAKING TIME AND SKILL LEVEL

This is a very straightforward, easy-to-make project—a sheet or two of thin cardboard, and a short time spent drawing and snipping, and the project is made. I would say that a 6- to 12-year-old could put this project together in about 10 to 20 minutes.

Cautions and adult help Although drawing and scissor-cutting are easy enough, younger children will need a bit of adult help when it comes to fitting and putting the mask together. Have a tryout on some scrap paper and see how it goes.

Be warned Masks are scary. If you leap out on grandma wearing this little number, you might make her jump; older people don't like shocks and surprises!

TOOLS AND MATERIALS

☐ A sheet of thin cardboard at about 12×18 inches. Best if it's a light colored, say, yellow, blue, or silver.
☐ A sheet of tracing paper to fit the card   ☐ A pencil and ruler
☐ A pair of scissors   ☐ A stapler   ☐ A few inches of double-sided sticky tape

MEASURE, MARK AND MAKE

1 Have a look at the project picture (FIG. 14-1) and the working drawings (FIGS. 14-2 and 14-3) and see how the mask is almost a helmet in that it covers the top of

Continued

Fig. 14-1 Moon Mask.

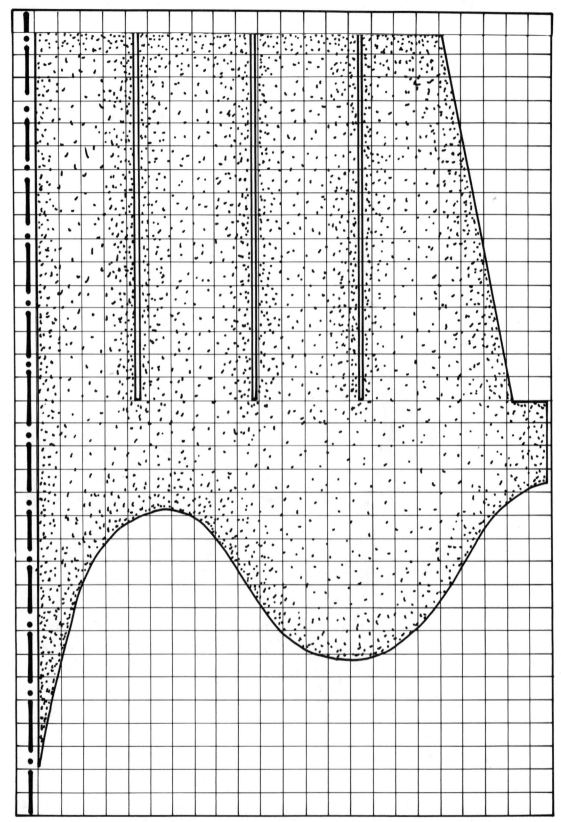

Fig. 14-2 Working drawing number 1. The scale is about 1 grid square to $1/4$ inch.

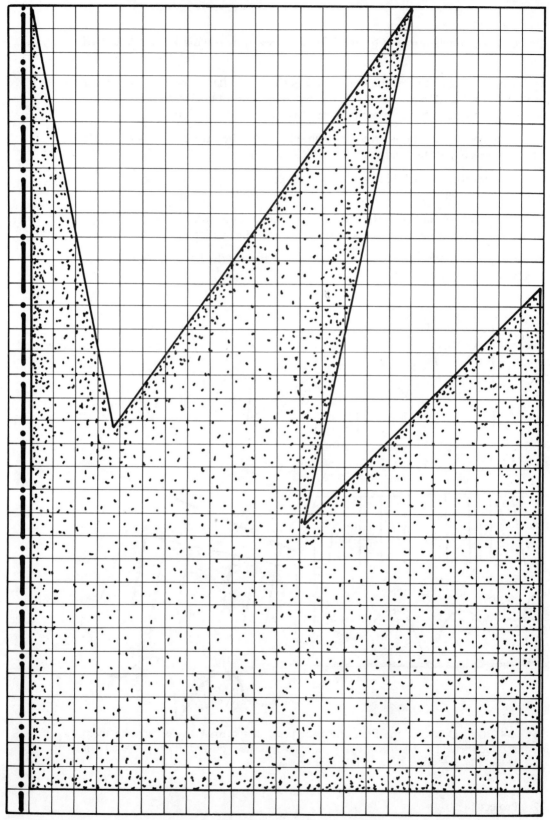

Fig. 14-3 Working drawing number 2. The scale is about 1 grid square to ¹/4 inch.

the head and comes down in front of the nose. See how the mask is made in two parts.

2   When you have studied the design and perhaps also had a tryout with a sheet of scrap paper/cardboard, trace off the two shapes and pencil-press-transfer the traced lines through to the working face of the card (FIG. 14-4 left).

3   Make sure that the transferred lines are clear, and then use the scissors to cut away the waste (FIG. 14-4 right).

4   Take the front piece, that is, the bit that goes over the top of the head and down the nose, and gather the seven flaps together (FIG. 14-5 right).

5   When you have adjusted the flaps so that the curved front of the mask stops short, just above your eyes, fix them through with the stapler.

6   Now, with an adult's help, fit the back piece around the back of the head and be ready to fit it at the sides.

Continued

Fig. 14-4 (Left) Draw out the front and back parts of the mask. If you arrange them carefully, you should be able to cut them out from one sheet of card. (Right) The cut out parts. Note the slots in the front section of the mask.

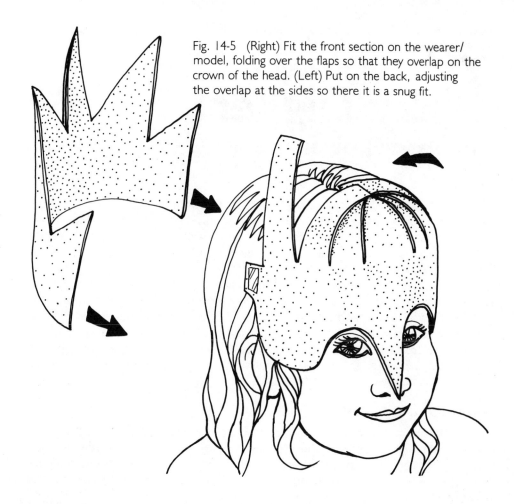

Fig. 14-5 (Right) Fit the front section on the wearer/model, folding over the flaps so that they overlap on the crown of the head. (Left) Put on the back, adjusting the overlap at the sides so there it is a snug fit.

7 Finally, when you have overlapped the back flaps over the front flaps to make a good total-mask fit, fix the flaps with tabs of masking tape (FIG. 14-5 left).

WATCH-POINTS AND FOLLOW-UPS

○ When you are choosing your cardboard, go for yellow or blue. Best of all, go for a shiny silver, foil-covered card.
○ You might need to have several trys before you get the fitting right
○ You could make the mask even more exciting and dramatic by having a green see-through plastic visor; ask an adult and see what they think.

15

Dizzy Digger
An elastic-powered toy

Dizzy Digger, the audacious Aussie is, without doubt, a really weird and wonderful, twirling whirling guy. Give his hat a hundred or so turns, set him down, and before you can say "Crazy kangaroos" and "Waltzing Matilda," his hat starts to slowly spin around. No folks, Dizzy Digger hasn't had too much sun, it's just that he's a playful character.

If you are looking to make a really unusual toy—one that will set your friends guessing, your neighbors grinning, and your parents sighing—then this is the project for you. Dizzy Digger is an enigma. Why does his hat turn? Why is he so funny? Who knows?

Funny, freakish, and fantastic, Dizzy could be yours. If you are fed up with dolls, teddy bears, toy soldiers, bikes, and all your other playthings, then I've got a feeling that this is the project for you!

MAKING TIME AND SKILL LEVEL

Although each of the various making stages are relatively simple, I think it fair to say the sum total of all the steps and stages make for a project that is quite difficult. Bearing in mind that most children will need a good deal of help and guidance along the way, I figure that 6- to 12-year-olds will be able to put this project together in 1 to 2 hours.

Cautions and adult help   This project is tricky because there's a lot going on. For example, when you come to pushing the elastic band through the bottle, and the stick through the band, and the band through the hat, the whole thing is likely to spring apart in your hands. You will need adult help when you come to putting the project together.

Be warned   Rubber bands, quick-set glues, needles, scissors, and sharp-edge plastics are all potentially dangerous—you do need to be careful. Best to set out the working area and have all the tools and materials carefully arranged so that they are all within easy reach. If you are organized, if you make sure that toddlers and pets are out of the way, and if you take each stage slowly, one little step at a time, then you won't have any problems.

TOOLS AND MATERIALS
☐ A medium-size plastic shampoo-type bottle
☐ A selection of rubber bands

Continued

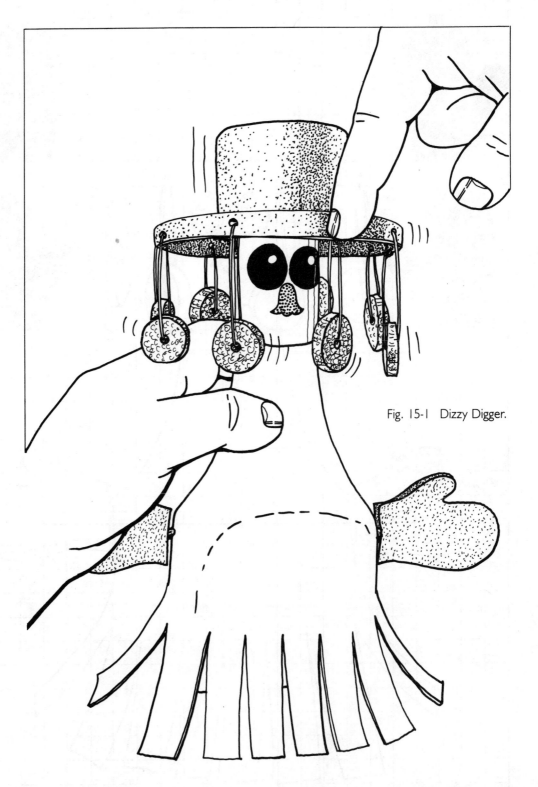

Fig. 15-1 Dizzy Digger.

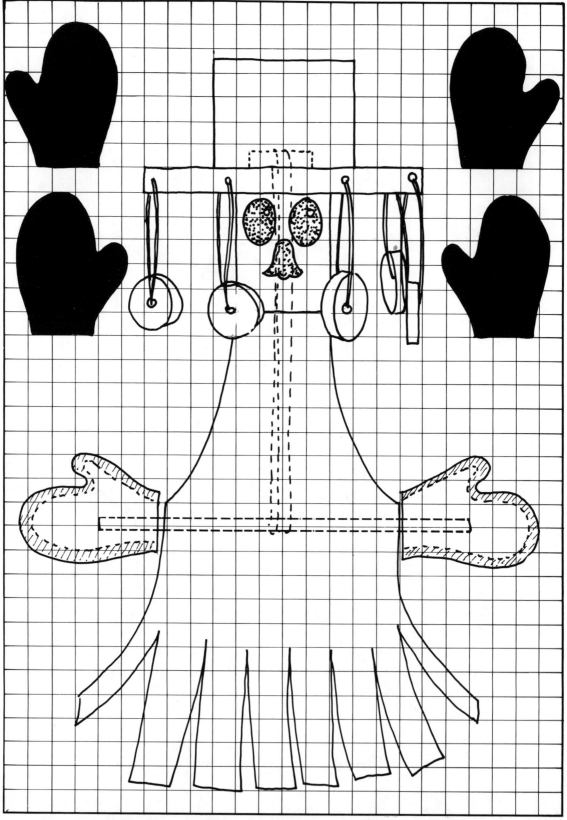

Fig. 15-2 Working drawing. The scale is about I grid square to ¼ inch.

- ☐ A flat plastic lid for the hat brim; perhaps from a milk powder container
- ☐ A wine-bottle cork ☐ A needle and thread ☐ A paper punch
- ☐ A tube of contact adhesive ☐ Odds and ends of colored paper
- ☐ A small plastic or cardboard drum for the top of the hat; we have used a dried herb container
- ☐ A small smear of wax furniture polish
- ☐ A short length of dowel; we have used an old paintbrush handle
- ☐ A junior hacksaw or an old saw-edge bread knife ☐ A pair of scissors

MEASURE, MARK AND MAKE

❙ Have a look at the project picture (FIG. 15-1) and the working drawing (FIG. 15-2), and see how Dizzy is powered by a rubber band that runs from the inside of the hat, down through the bottle to the dowel. See how, in use, the hat is turned so that the rubber band is wound up. Note the various washers and sticks.

Continued

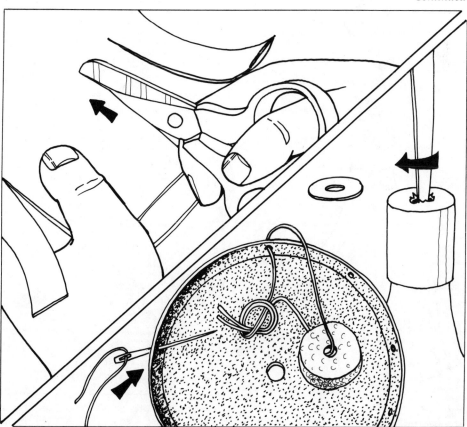

Fig. 15-3 (Top Left) Cut the slots in the bottle from the base; travel right around the bottle, spacing the slots evenly. (Bottom Right) Score a hole on the top of the bottle with scissors, make the washer, then drill a large hole in the center of the hat rim and eight small holes around the edge. Thread the corks on.

2 Ask an adult to cut and prepare the plastic bottle; the bottom needs to be removed and the sides of the bottle need to be cut to make the evenly spaced slotted fringe (FIG. 15-3 top).

3 Ask an adult to help you push a hole through the soft plastic lid and to make a washer; the holes in the lid and the washer need to be smooth-edged and large enough to take the rubber band, and the washer must be no bigger than the top of the bottle (FIG. 15-3 bottom right).

4 Punch about eight holes around the rim of the soft plastic hat brim, saw the cork into eight slices, and use the needle and thread to thread-and-hang the slices of cork around the brim of the hat (FIG. 15-3 bottom left).

Continued

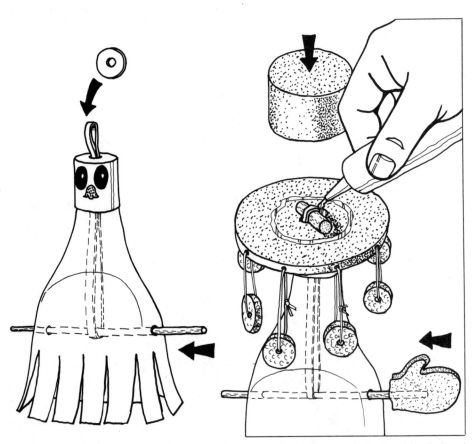

Fig. 15-4 (Left) Thread the rubber band down through the bottle. Push the old paintbrush through the holes on the side, passing through the loop of the rubber band. Thread the washer on. (Right) Thread the hat rim on, pass a small stick/dowel through to loop at the other end of the rubber band, and glue to the hat rim top. Glue the top of the hat and the hands on.

5 At a point about three-quarters of the way down from Dizzy's head, make an "arm" hole on either side of the plastic container; push the dowel through the holes so that the "arms" stick out of each side.

6 Select a good, fat rubber band, remove and reset the dowel so the band is held, and then push the rubber band up through the body of the bottle, through the lid, and on through the small plastic washer (FIG. 15-4 left). Smear a small amount of wax polish over the washer.

7 Push the rubber band on up through the hat brim and hold it in place with a short length of dowel and a blob or two of quick-set glue (FIG. 15-4 right).

8 Finally, stick the top of the hat on the brim, the thin cardboard hands on the ends of the arm dowel, and the colored paper eyes and nose on the face (FIG. 15-4 right).

WATCH-POINTS AND FOLLOW-UPS

❍ When you are choosing your bottle, go for one that is made of soft, easy-to-bend, non-splinter plastic.
❍ Make sure that the bottle is well washed out, clean, and dry.
❍ To speed up the hole-making stages, you could ask an adult to make all the holes with an electric drill and a 3/8-inch drill bit.
❍ Not all adhesives are plastic-friendly, ask your shop for a clear quick-set plastic-to-wood glue.

16

Whistle Warbler
A paper whistle

When I was a little kid, I used to turn my paper bus tickets into bird whistles! I say whistles, but really they ought to have been called screechers. The moment I had my ticket, I would fold it in half, make a little hole in the fold, and then presto! I had a whistle. The best bit about these whistles, was the loud, piercing shrieks that they sent out when they were held between two fingers and blown. They made just about the loudest, the scratchiest, the nastiest noise in the whole wide world—a bit like a crow with a sore throat, or a raven in pain, or even a hungry vulture. Of course, the moment the whistle was blown, all the people on the bus would whip round in horror and surprise; it was really good fun.

But, anyway, if you are looking to make an update of my antisocial ticket whistle, then this is the project for you.

MAKING TIME AND SKILL LEVEL

This is a very basic easy-to-make project—a fold in a piece of thin cardboard, a snip or two with a pair of scissors, and the project is three-parts made. I would say that most 6- to 12-year-olds could have their whistles made in about 15 minutes.

Cautions and adult help You won't need adult help with this one; it's safe and it's easy.

Be warned Some folk are really upset by unexpected loud noises; it's worth noting that once or twice the bus driver and the passengers were so annoyed by my screechings that they told me in no uncertain terms to mind my manners.

TOOLS AND MATERIALS

☐ A piece of thin colored cardboard about 9×3 inches
☐ A piece of tracing paper to fit the card
☐ A few small scraps of different-colored cardboard
☐ A pencil and ruler ☐ A pair of scissors ☐ A glue stick

MEASURE, MARK AND MAKE

I Have a look at the project picture (FIG. 16-1) and the working drawings (FIG. 16-2), and see how the bird whistle is no more than a little bird-shape fold of card with a few folds. Note the sound hole at the beak and the little bits and pieces of colored card appliqué.

Continued

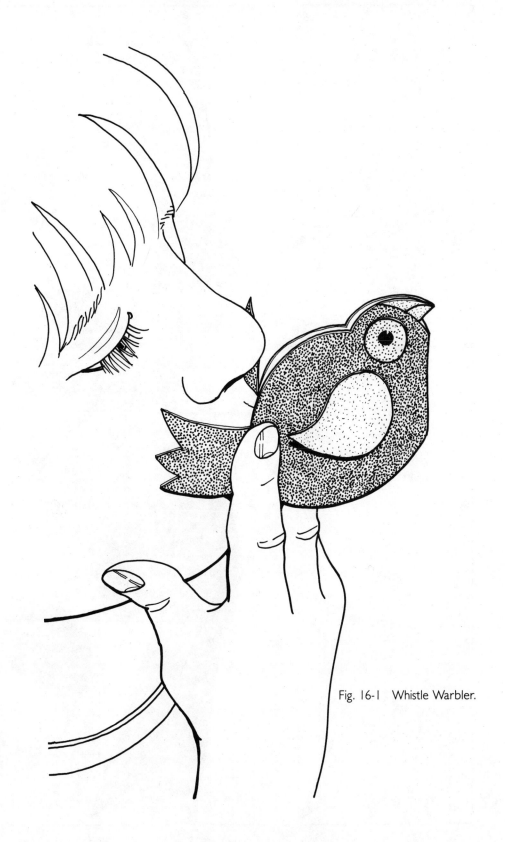

Fig. 16-1   Whistle Warbler.

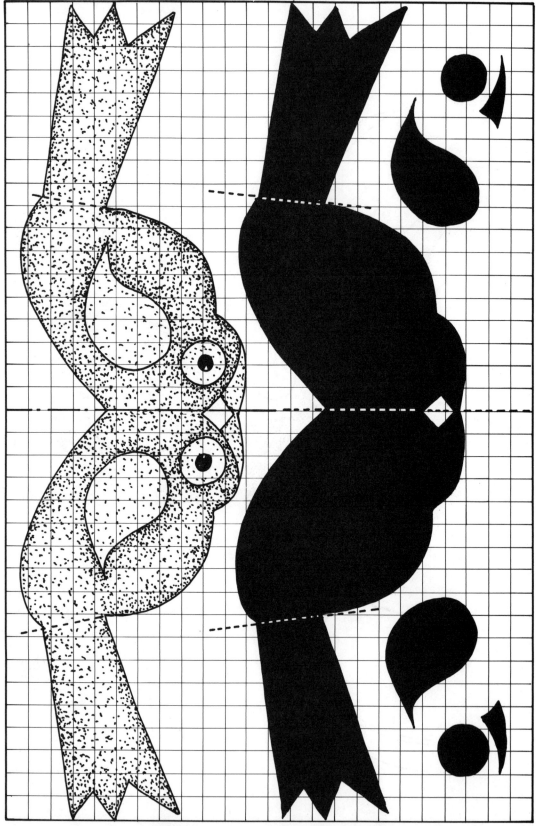

Fig. 16-2 Working drawing. The scale is about 1 grid square to ¼ inch.

2 Trace off the lines of the design and carefully pencil-press-transfer the main bird form through to the best face of the 9-×-3-inch strip of colored cardboard, and the wings, eye, and beak details through to the little scraps of colored cardboard (FIG. 16-3 top).

3 Mark in the position of wings, eyes, and beak and then cut out all the little shapes that go to make up the project (FIG. 16-3 bottom). Don't forget to cut out the little beak hole.

4 With the beak-to-beak cutout flat down on the worksurface, glue the wings, eyes, and beaks in place, and use a felt-tip pen to line in the eye and beak details (FIG. 16-4 top).

Continued

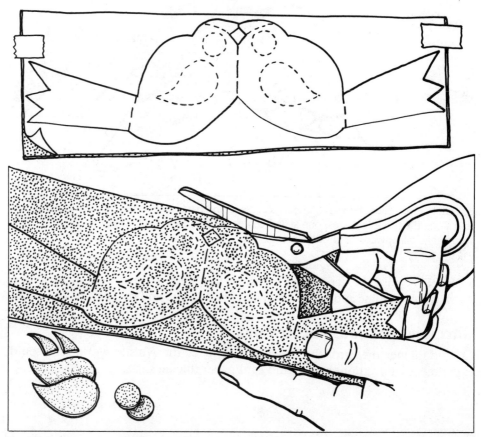

Fig. 16-3 (Top) Pencil-press-transfer the lines of the design onto colored card. (Bottom) Cut around the outside of the drawn line. You will need a large piece of card for the bird's body, a small piece of yellow card for the wings and beak, and two blue circles for the eyes.

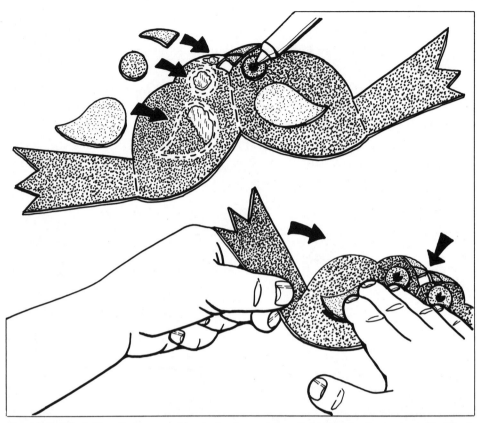

Fig. 16-4 (Top) Glue the eyes and beaks in place and partially glue the two wings. (Bottom) Fold along the three fold lines, one at the center of back area and two at the tail/body area. Spread the tail upwards and outwards.

5 Finally, crease the card along the three fold lines, so that the bird is folded down the center line and so the two tails are folded up and out (FIG. 16-4 bottom).

WATCH-POINTS AND FOLLOW-UPS

○ The thinner the card, the easier it is to make the whistle work; you could experiment with various shapes and card/paper thicknesses.

All in a Whorl
String printing book-cover paper

Round and round they go—snail shells, fingerprints, spiral staircases, the lines on a record—they are all good examples of whorl patterns. Characteristically the lines in a whorl start at the center, then gradually go around and around, and out and out, all the while getting bigger and bigger. Look around you and see how many whorl patterns you can find in nature; try for starters looking at flower heads, looking at leaves growing up the stems of some flowers, and looking at fossils. Circles within circles, curved lines going around and around one within another—whorls make amazing patterns!

Okay then, so you are looking to hand-print a personalized book-cover paper. What better than winding a length of string up so as to make a classic whorl form and then to print an overall whorl pattern? Beautiful!

MAKING TIME AND SKILL LEVEL

Easy-to-make, string printing is the perfect technique for quickly printing sheets of book-cover paper. From start to finish, a 6- to 12-year-old could have this project all wrapped in about 20 to 60 minutes.

Cautions and adult help   Safe and easy—we don't think that you are going to need adult help with this one. Let your parents know what you want to do, and see what they advise.

Be warned   Acrylic paint dries very fast; cover the working area with newspaper, wear old clothes, and wash the brushes as soon as you are finished with them.

TOOLS AND MATERIALS
- [ ] A large sheet of white paper to be printed
- [ ] A cardboard disk about 2½ inches in diameter, perhaps from a food jar lid.
- [ ] A length of fat, hairy string   ☐ A tube of quick-set balsa cement/glue
- [ ] A roll of masking tape   ☐ A few scraps of paper and card
- [ ] A pot/tube of acrylic paint; best to go for a strong bright color.
- [ ] A pair of scissors   ☐ A plate

MEASURE, MARK AND MAKE

1 Have a look at the project picture (FIG. 17-1) and the working drawing (FIG. 17-2) and see how the whorl prints are set out in staggered lines to form a good overall design.

2 Take the string and the cardboard disk, put a blob of glue at the center of the disk, and then gradually stick-and-place the string around and around so as to build a whorl design (FIG. 17-3 top).

3 When the whorl of string has been well placed on the card, and when the glue is dry, turn the disk over so that it is string-side down, and fit a card-and-sticky-tape loop handle (FIG. 17-3 bottom).

Continued

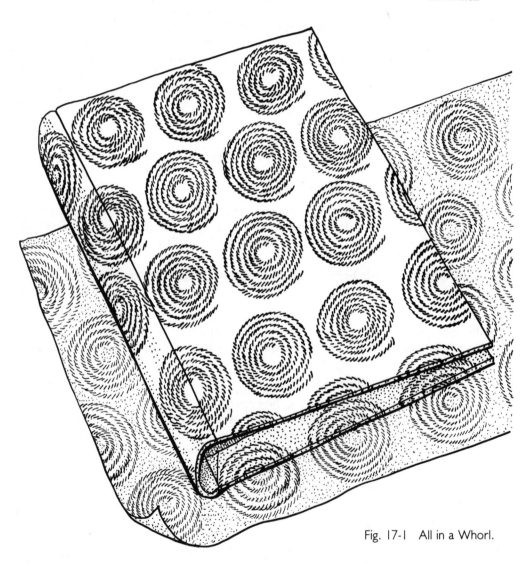

Fig. 17-1 All in a Whorl.

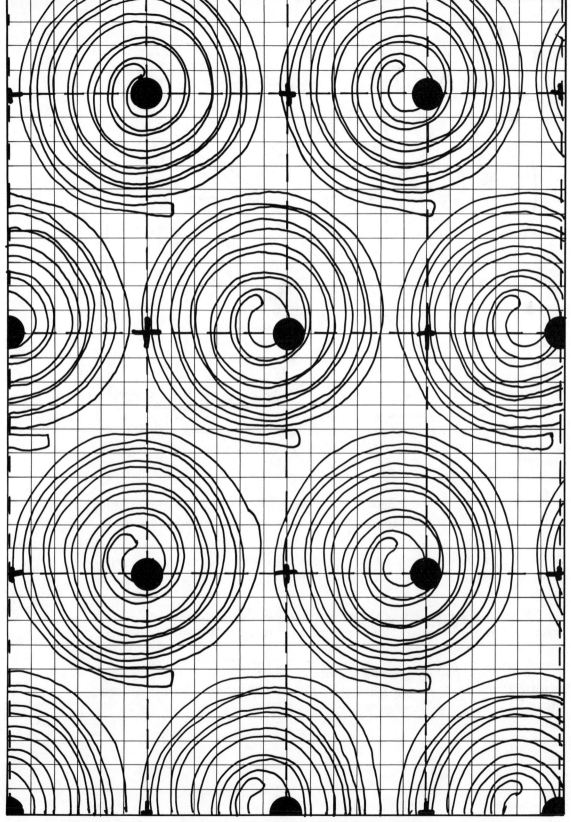

Fig. 17-2   Working drawing. The scale is about 1 grid square to ¹/₄ inch.

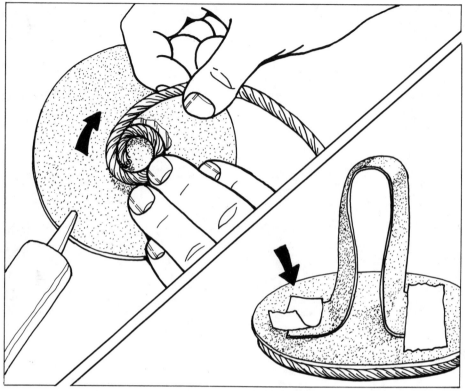

Fig. 17-3 (Top Left) Dab glue on the card and hold the string in place on the glued area until it stays put — then move around, spiralling outward, until all the card is covered. (Bottom Right) Tape a card loop on the back of the block.

4 Have another look at our design, just to see how the individual whorl prints are set out, then cover the worksurface with newspaper and smooth out the pieces of paper to be printed (FIG. 17-4).

5 Brush a small amount of thick acrylic color backwards and forwards over the plate, and then press the printing disks firmly down into the paint (FIG. 17-4 top left).

6 Lift the printing disk out of the paint, make sure that you know where you want the prints to be placed, and then print off two whorls (FIG. 17-4 bottom right).

7 And so you continue—pressing the disk in the paint, printing once, printing twice, pressing the disk in the paint, and so on until the overall design has been printed.

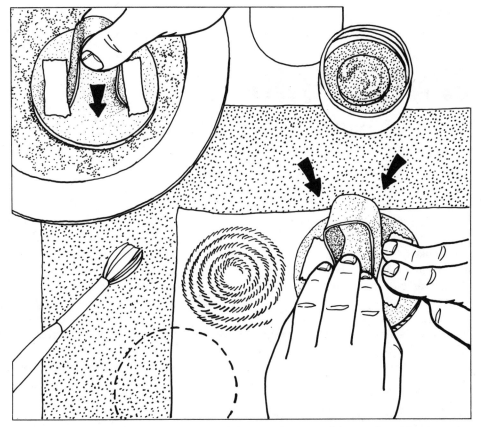

Fig. 17-4 Dab the printing block into the colors on the saucer/plate and position it on the paper to be printed. Press down firmly, and pull the block upwards and away after the print has been made. Note: the broken line circle shows the printing position of the first print on the next row. Spread newspaper under the printing paper to keep the table clean.

WATCH-POINTS AND FOLLOW-UPS

○ When you come to choosing your string, best go for a natural, hairy, absorbent yarn like sisal.

○ The cardboard disk really needs to be water-resistant—okay if you are using a disk from a food jar, but otherwise, cut a disk from card and give it a coat of glue or paint and let it dry. Do this well before you start gluing down the string.

○ The paint needs to be thick and non-runny, and the paper to be printed must be absorbent. Check this out before you start printing.

18

Swiss Snip
A Swiss paper-cuts greeting card

Paper cutting is a wonderfully direct and easy craft—a sheet of paper, a pair of scissors, and few minutes spent snipping, folding, and cutting, and before you can wink, you will have made a paper-cut decoration. Paper cutting is a traditional craft that is done all over the world. In Japan they make paper sculptures, in China they make tissue-paper kites, in Poland they make color paper banners and motifs, and so on; each country has its own paper-cutting craft tradition. And so it is that in Switzerland, they make uniquely delicate lace-like tracery pictures.

These small hand-size black paper pictures are jam-packed full of all the images that we now think of as being Swiss. There are horses and stags, cows with bells, love-hearts and rabbits, trees and Swiss-type log cabins—all worked in mirror image silhouette. Beautiful!

If you want to make a delicate, fragile, papercut pictures, this is the project for you.

MAKING TIME AND SKILL LEVEL

Although making paper-cuts is relatively easy, I think it fair to say that this rather delicate design is aimed at older children. A careful-cutting 10- to 12-year-old will be able to make this project in about an hour.

If you are looking for a good fire-side craft project—one that you can sleepily do on a wet and wintery Sunday afternoon—then you won't go wrong with paper cutting.

Cautions and adult help   This project is easy. If you know how to fold paper and how to manage a pair of scissors, then I'd say you can go it alone without adult help.

Be warned   You may be old enough to know that scissors can be dangerous, but watch out for pets and younger brothers and sisters; put the scissors away when you have finished with them.

TOOLS AND MATERIALS

☐ A sheet of thin black paper at about $4^{1}/4 \times 4^{1}/4$ inches; best to use a sheet of white paper that is printed black on one side.

☐ A sheet of thin colored card at about $10^{1}/2 \times 8^{1}/2$ inches. Go for a strong color like dark green.

☐ A pencil and ruler   ☐ A sheet of tracing paper
☐ A small amount of masking tape or low-tack sticky tape
☐ A pair of small scissors
☐ A tube/stick of clear quick/set paper adhesive

MEASURE, MARK AND MAKE

I   Have a look at the project picture (FIG. 18-1) and the pattern page (FIG. 18-2), and study how the black paper is folded in half and how it is carefully cut and worked with scissors. Note how the mirror-image design faces the center fold.

Continued

Fig. 18-1 Swiss Snip.

Fig. 18-2 Working drawing. The scale is about 1 grid square to ¼ inch.

2 Fold the sheet of black-faced paper in half so that the black face is innermost, and trace off the lines of the design (FIG. 18-3 left).

3 Position the tracing on the book-folded paper so that the horse looks towards the center-line, secure the tracing with a few tabs of sticky tape, and carefully pencil-press-transfer the traced lines through to the white working face of the paper (FIG. 18-3 top right).

4 Remove the tracing paper, shade in the areas of that need to be cut away, secure the folded paper with small pieces of sticky tape, then set to work cutting away the windows of waste (FIG. 18-3 bottom right). When you have swiftly removed the main piece of waste, cut in towards the drawn lines.

5 When you come to cutting away the very smallest windows of waste, carefully fold the paper, nip-and-snip a small "V," then enter the scissors and cut out towards the drawn lines (FIG. 18-4 top).

Continued

Fig. 18-3 (Left) Cut out the square of colored paper and fold in half so that the colored area is inside. Trace off half the design and tape this tracing over the paper. (Top Right) Pencil-press-transfer the drawing onto the paper. (Bottom Right) Using very small pieces of tape, secure the folded paper and cut out all the main areas—it may help to shade in all areas to be removed.

6 Finally, when you have made a good paper-cut design, fold the sheet of colored cardboard in half to make a book-fold that measures about 10×8 inches, draw in a few faint pencil guidelines at side and center, and then stick the paper-cut down into position (FIG. 18-4 bottom).

WATCH-POINTS AND FOLLOW-UPS

❍ If you can't find a sheet of paper that is white on one side and black on the other, brush black ink over one side of a sheet of white typing paper.

❍ When you come to gluing the finished paper-cut down on the card, set the workpiece black-side down on a sheet of newspaper and smear on the smallest possible amount of glue. Work out from center towards the side edges.

❍ You need two guidelines on the front of the card, one down the center and one about 1¼ inches down from the top edge.

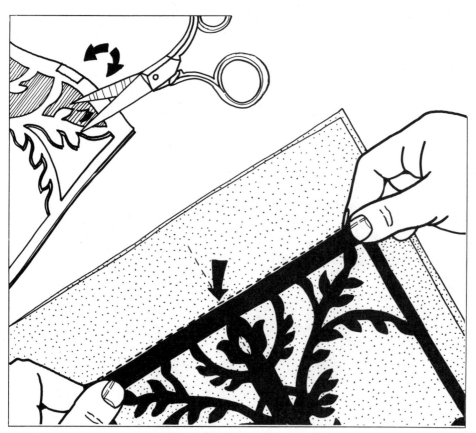

Fig. 18-4 (Top Left) To cut out small area, fold the paper cut and nip and snip a small V-shaped cut. Then insert the scissors into this cut and travel toward the edges of the waste areas. (Bottom) To get the paper cut straight when mounting it on a card, draw faint center and top lines in pencil on the card, then use these lines as a guide.

Cut-and-Cover
Decorating a box with découpage

Découpage is the fancy French name for the craft of decorating surfaces with paper cutouts, meaning paper prints, pictures, and illustrations. The object to be decorated is first cleaned, rubbed down, and painted; the prints and illustrations are chosen and carefully cut out; the cutouts are glued onto the surface to be decorated; and finally, the finished design is covered with at least three coats of clear yacht varnish. The end result of all this snipping, cutting, gluing, and varnishing is a deep-shine decoration that looks as if it has been cleverly painted or transferred.

So, if you have, say, a box, chest, cupboard, screen, or whatever that needs to be decorated, and if you have a pile of favorite magazines, pictures, photographs, and prints that are looking for a home, now's the time to make a découpage.

MAKING TIME AND SKILL LEVEL

This is one of those projects that is best worked over several days or even weeks. You can spend time searching out prints, then at a later stage you can cut the prints out, and at a later-still stage you can stick the cutouts down and put varnish over them. Having said that, I would guess that from the first scissor-snip to the last lick of varnish, a 8- to 12-year-old kid could, with a little help, easily make this project in a couple of hours.

Cautions and adult help   Although paper cutting and varnishing are a relatively easy single-handed task, you could speed up the project by making it an assembly-line-type operation. So, for example, your dad could paint the object, your brother or sister could do all the cutting out, then you could do all the sticking down and varnishing. It could be a whole heap of family fun!

Be warned   Paint is sticky, scissors are snippy, and varnish is tricky. Be sure to carefully prepare your working area by putting down plenty of newspaper and by being ready with old cloths, water, and turpentine.

TOOLS AND MATERIALS
- [ ] A small wooden box to decorate
- [ ] A small saucer or plate
- [ ] A small pair of scissors
- [ ] A can of clear yacht varnish
- [ ] Acrylic paint in colors to suit
- [ ] Brushes
- [ ] A collection of magazines
- [ ] A small amount of white PVA-type glue

MEASURE, MARK AND MAKE

1 Have a look at the project picture (FIG. 19-1) and the working drawings (FIG. 19-2), and see how the cutouts are selected and mounted so that they all relate to a set design theme. Aim to collect cutouts that look as if they belong together.

2 Spend time collecting all your magazine, comic, and cartoon pictures. Group them according to type, size, and overall color.

3 Make sure that the surface to be decorated is clean, sound, and dry. Decide on a suitable background color, then lay on a couple of good coats of quick-drying acrylic paint (FIG. 19-3 top).

4 When the paint is completely dry, carefully cut out the pictures, patterns, and designs, and have a trial dry-run (FIG. 19-3 bottom). Experiment by placing the cutouts first this way, then that way, until you have a good design.

5 When you come to sticking the cutouts, set them face-down in a little pool of PVA glue, and use a brush to work the glue well into the back (FIG. 19-4 top).

6 Turn the glue-soaked picture right-side-up, place it carefully in position on the box, and brush the best face with PVA glue and a few drops of water (FIG. 19-4 bottom).

7 And so you continue until all the cutouts have all been well soaked in glue, carefully arranged, and brushed into place.

8 When the glue is completely dry, lay on at least two coats of clear varnish.

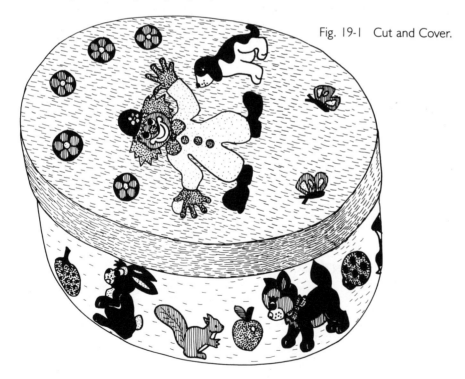

Fig. 19-1 Cut and Cover.

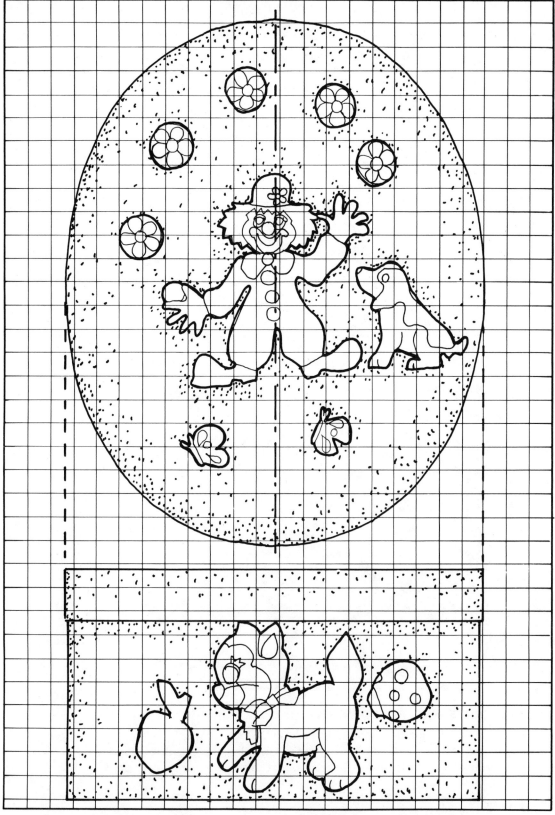

Fig. 19-2 Working drawing. The scale is about 1 grid square per ¼ inch.

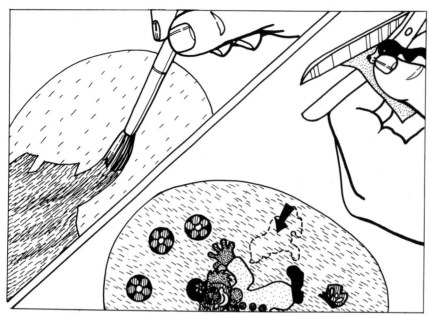

Fig. 19-3 (Top Left) Paint the box evenly, make the lid green and the rest of the box yellow. (Bottom Right) Cut out all the motifs and arrange them on the box.

Fig. 19-4 (Top) Make a water and glue mixture in a saucer and dampen each motif on both sides. (Bottom) Carefully place the motif onto the glue and brush glue over the surface, smoothing out any creases.

WATCH-POINTS AND FOLLOW-UPS

○ Make sure you use a quick-drying, water-based, PVA-type glue.
○ Don't worry if the wet glued-down cutouts look milky, the glue dries out clear.
○ Before you start the varnishing, make sure that the glue is completely dry.

20
Myth Mask
A Haida Indian mask

The Indians on the Northwest Pacific coast of Canada and Alaska were lucky and unique. The Kwakkiutl, the Tsimshian, the Salish, and the Haida Indians were lucky because they lived in an area so rich in food they only needed to spend a couple of months each year hunting and fishing, and they were unique because, once they had put by enough food for the winter, they spent the rest of the year dancing, acting out myth plays, and making beautiful craft objects. Because they were surrounded by huge forests of easy-to-carve cedar trees and were well fed, they were able to spend most days working and carving wood. They built large houses, they carved the biggest totem poles in the world, and of course, they carved the most wonderful masks. What a life!

If you want to make a really good Indian mask look-a-like, then just read on.

MAKING TIME AND SKILL LEVEL

This is a pretty straightforward project. I would say that a 7- to 12-year-old could have the mask made in about 20 to 40 minutes.

Cautions and adult help You might need a little help making the eye holes and fitting the cord ties, but, really, I would say this is a project you can manage on your own.

Be warned Make the eye holes well before you put the mask on. *Keep the scissors away from your eyes!*

TOOLS AND MATERIALS

☐ A sheet of medium-thick cardboard about 12 × 12 inches; it needs to be pastel-colored on both sides and big enough to cover your face.
☐ A sheet of tracing paper to fit the card   ☐ A pencil and ruler
☐ A pair of scissors   ☐ A pack of colored felt-tip pens
☐ A roll of sticky tape   ☐ A piece of soft cord about 24 inches long

MEASURE, MARK AND MAKE

I First have a good look at the project picture (FIG. 20-1) and the pattern page (FIG. 20-2), and see how the cardboard mask is cut and worked. See how the long nose-piece is folded down over the face, and how the side flaps need to folded over for the tie cords.

Continued

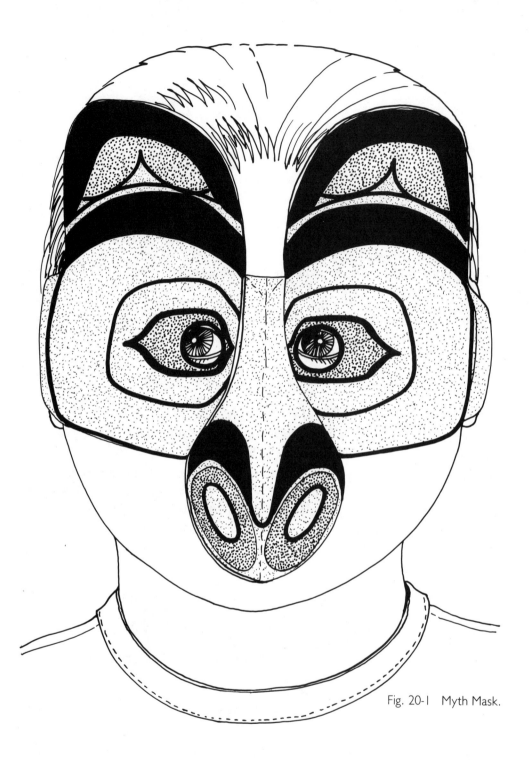

Fig. 20-1   Myth Mask.

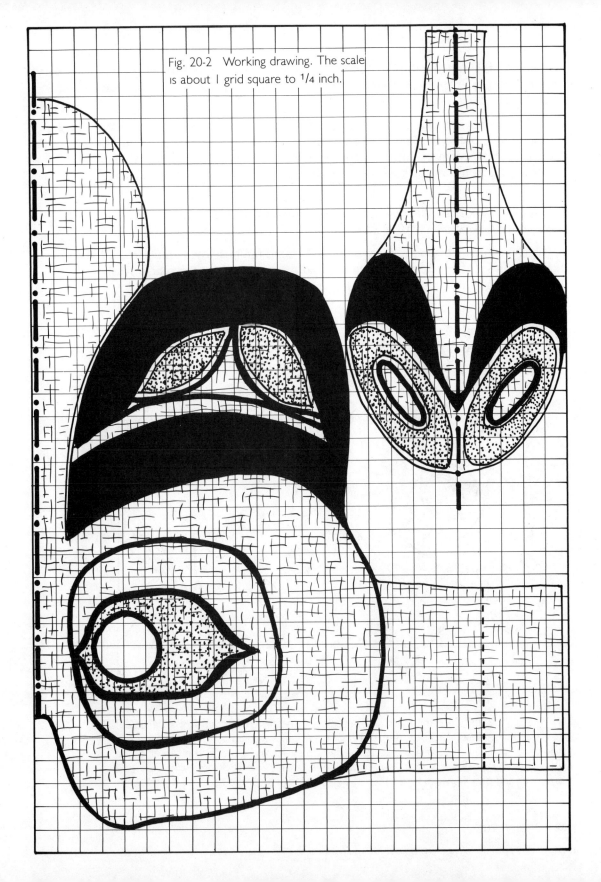

Fig. 20-2 Working drawing. The scale is about 1 grid square to 1/4 inch.

2   Trace off the design and pencil-press-transfer the traced lines through to the working face of the cardboard; don't bother to trace the nose patterns on this side of the card.

3   When you have drawn in all the lines, cut away the large areas of waste, and cut round the nose so that it is separate from the ears. When you come to cutting the two eye holes, start by cutting a small nick in the center of the eye, then carefully work the points of the scissors out and around towards the cutting line (FIG. 20-3 top).

4   Turn the mask right-side-down, and pencil-press-transfer the pattern lines that make up the nose design (FIG. 20-3 bottom).

5   With the mask face-up on the worksurface, bend the nose over-and-down so that you can see the patterns, and then spend time blocking in the whole mask design with the felt-tip colors (FIG. 20-4 top).

Continued

Fig. 20-3   (Top Left) Trace the mask and pencil-press the design through to the card. Cut away the waste areas, separate the nose from the ears, and cut away the eye sockets (shaded area). This can be difficult. To make this job easier, cut a nick in the center of the socket first and work the scissors out towards the cutting line. (Bottom Right) Turn the mask over and pencil-press-transfer the lines of the design onto the nose.

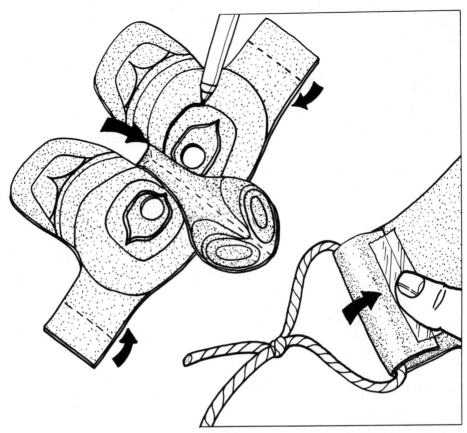

Fig. 20-4 (Top Left) Fold over the nose and crease it down its length along the center-line. Color in the shapes, using felt-tip pens. (Bottom Right) To make the ties (one on each side of the mask) loop and tie a piece of cord, place it along the crease line on the back of the mask, and fold and tape the tabs to make a firm joint.

6 Finally, when you come to making the two cord ties—one for each side of the mask—cut the 24 inches of cord into half, tie a loop in each end, slide the loops on the side tabs, and then fix with sticky tape (FIG. 20-4 bottom).

WATCH-POINTS AND FOLLOW-UPS

○ If you want to make sure that the mask is symmetrical, you could fold the card in-half down the center-line, and clear away the waste by cutting through two thicknesses of card at the same-time—you need to have strong hands.

○ If you like the idea of mask-making, you could follow on from this project and try making a paper-mâché mask.

○ You could look at the other mask-making project in this book (Project 14), and make a helmet-type mask—one that fits over the top of the head.

21
High Flyer
A kite

Swooping and falling, diving and twisting, curving and rolling, kite flying is really one of the most exciting activities that I can think of. To watch your kite high up in the sky and to feel it tugging and twitching at the end of the line—it's a great feeling. And the best thing about kite flying is that you don't have to be rich or famous to take part. Of course this is not to say that you *can't* be rich or famous. Did you know that Benjamin Franklin used a kite in his experiments? That Franklin Cody the American showman flew kites? That the American flyers Wilbur and Orville Wright started their famous glider experiments by flying kites? And that Alexander Graham Bell spent time inventing kites?

Ok, so why don't you make a kite and get out there and join in the fun. Is it a bird? Is it a plane? No! It's a High Flyer Kite!

MAKING TIME AND SKILL LEVEL

Although this particular kite isn't in any way difficult, all kites do need to be made slowly and carefully. I would say that, with a bit of help, an 8- to 12-year-old could have this project made and flying in the space of a morning.

Cautions and adult help   You will need adult help—it's not that the project is tricky, it's just that there are too many things to manage on your own.

Be warned   Kite flying can be fun, but it can also be dangerous. Never fly your kite in the rain, stay away from busy roads, raging rivers, and low-flying aircraft, and, most important of all, *stay away from overhead powerlines!*

TOOLS AND MATERIALS

☐ Two ¹/₂-inch-diameter dowels, one 36 inches long, the other 24 inches long.
☐ A sheet of strong brown wrapping paper at 36×24 inches; best if it's a light brown color.
☐ A ball of fine, strong cotton twine   ☐ A small piece of sandpaper
☐ A pencil and tape measure   ☐ A pair of scissors
☐ A roll of double-sided sticky tape   ☐ A tube of clear quick-set glue
☐ A large, giant-size black felt-tip marker pen
☐ A strong brass curtain or key ring   ☐ A plastic sheet
☐ At least 200 yards of fishing line with reel

Fig. 21-1   High Flyer.

Fig. 21-2 Working drawing. The scale is about 1 grid square to 1 inch.

MEASURE, MARK AND MAKE

1 Have a look at the project picture (FIG. 21-1) and the working drawing (FIG. 21-2) and see how the kit is made from strong brown wrapping paper, two 1/2-inch-diameter dowels, and thin twine. Note how the kite measures about 36 inches from top to tail and 24 inches from side to side.

2 When you have studied all the sizes and proportions, and when you have gathered together all your tools and materials, take a pencil and ruler and find the center point or the halfway point on each dowel.

3 With the dowels crossed at the center points, dampen a length of cotton twine, and lash and bind the central cross (FIG. 21-3 top left and right). When the cotton dries out, the knot will tighten up.

4 When the lashing is tight and dry, make sure that the knot stays put by covering it with quick-set glue (FIG. 21-3 bottom left).

Continued

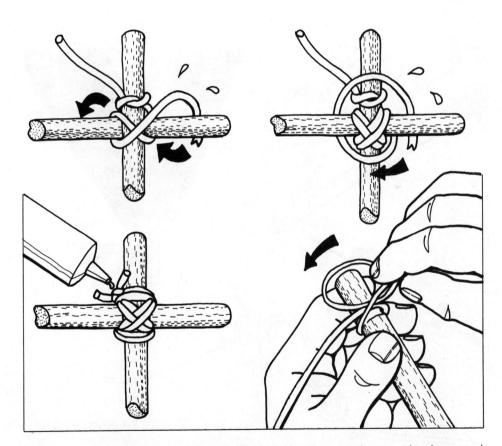

Fig. 21-3 (Top, left to right; and Bottom Left) Lashing the central cross, using damp cord, and fixing it with glue. (Bottom Right) Making the clove hitch knot to secure the frame line, note the slight indentation near the end of the spar, to stop the line slipping down.

5 Use the sandpaper to make a little "neck" about ½ inch in from the end of each of the cross arms, then take the twine and go from arm to arm, tying on the frame line (FIG. 21-3 bottom right and FIG. 21-2 bottom right).

6 With the crossed dowels held by the taut frame line, set the diamond-shaped kite down on the brown paper and use it as a pattern to cut out the sail. Allow a 1-inch-wide all around margin for sticking over the frame line.

7 Roll and fold the 1-inch-wide margin over the line, and fix it with strips of double-sided sticky tape (FIG. 21-4 left).

8 To make a bridle, tie a length of strong twine from the head-and tail ends of the main dowel (FIG. 21-4 right). Cut back the sail cover so that the string doesn't rub, and reinforce the paper edge with a piece of sticky tape.

9 Loop the brass ring onto the bridle and tie it onto the main flying line (FIG. 21-4 bottom middle).

Continued

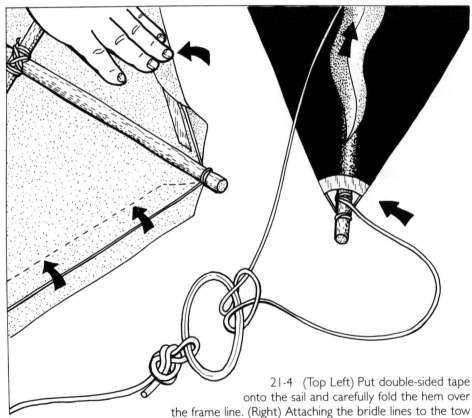

21-4 (Top Left) Put double-sided tape onto the sail and carefully fold the hem over the frame line. (Right) Attaching the bridle lines to the tow ring, so that the angle of the kite to the wind can be adjusted. Lastly attaching the flying line to the tow ring.

10 Use the black felt-tip pen to draw in the sun design (FIG. 21-2).

11 Finally, make a long tail by cutting a plastic sheet into 2-inch wide strips and sticking the strips together with sticky tape; the tail needs to be about 20 feet long (FIG. 21-1).

WATCH-POINTS AND FOLLOW-UPS

○ If the kite starts to unexpectedly buck or swoop in flight, try altering the position of the brass ring and/or making the tail longer.

○ You will need at least 200 yards of strong nylon fishing line for a flying line. Make sure that the end of the line is tied to a reel.

○ When you are flying the kite, best wear gloves and a pair of sunglasses.

22

Candle Cans
A tin-punch lantern

A camp fire, a wagon train, log cabins, horses, cattle, cowboys bedding down for the night, and the warm, soft glow of candle lanterns—wonderful! Of course, life in the Wild West wasn't all guitars, singing under the stars, and cozy camp fires, it was also hard and difficult. For example, if a cowboy or a homesteader wanted anything out of the ordinary, he just had to get down to work and make it. And so it was, they didn't throw away such items as bean cans, but rather, they washed them out, fiddled about with a knife, pliers, and wire, and turned them into just about everything from pierced tin box panels, through to belt buckles, mirror surrounds, and candle lanterns.

If you would like to make yourself a genuine Wild West cowboy candle lantern, a really exciting lantern for your next camp or late night barbecue, this is the project for you.

MAKING TIME AND SKILL LEVEL

Although this is a pretty straight forward and easy-to-make project, I would say that because of the sharp tin, it is best suited for older children, or for children working alongside adults. A 10- to 12-year-old will have the lantern made and working in about 25 to 35 minutes.

Cautions and adult help   Don't just rush into the kitchen and start work on the first tin can that comes to hand, have a talk to an adult and ask for their help and advice.

Be warned   No problems when the lantern is finished, because the sharp edges are out of harm's ways, but in between times, you will have to be very careful not to cut your fingers. *Tin is very sharp—wear thick leather work gloves!*

TOOLS AND MATERIALS

- [ ] A medium-size tin can; we have used a syrup tin, one with a pop-off lid and a safe-to-touch rolled rim.
- [ ] A length of thin coat hanger wire   [ ] A pair of pliers
- [ ] A "V" point can opener   [ ] The use of a couple of forks
- [ ] A small foil-cup nightlight
- [ ] A small tin of matte black heat-resistant paint; the type used to paint motorbike engines
- [ ] A small paint brush   [ ] A tube of clear quick-set glue

MEASURE, MARK AND MAKE

1 Have a look at the project picture (FIG. 22-1) and the working drawing page (FIG. 22-2), and see how the lantern is made and put together. See how the holes are punched around the rim and base, and how the wire handle is bent and fixed.

Continued

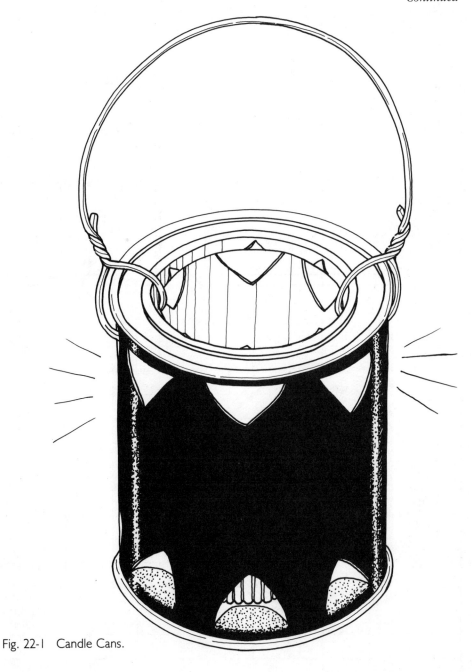

Fig. 22-1 Candle Cans.

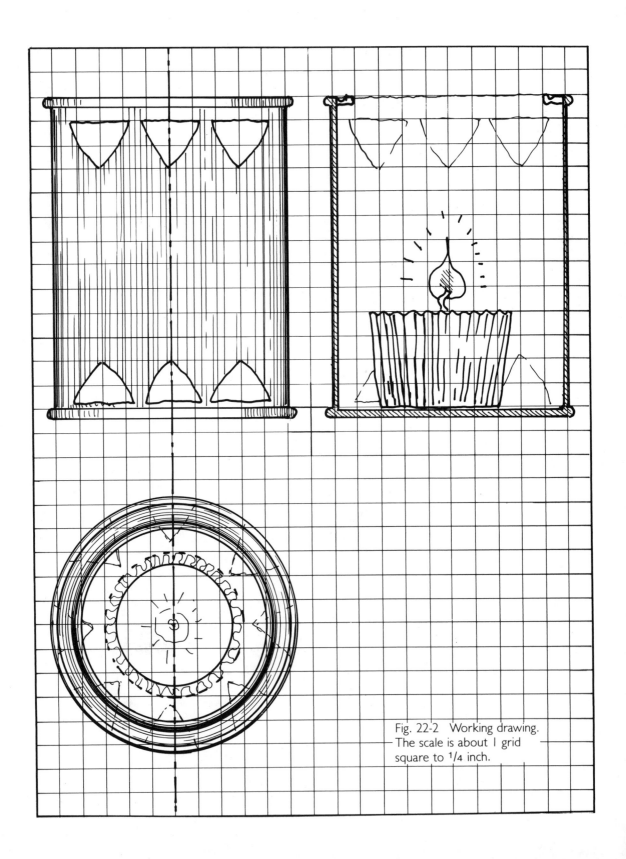

Fig. 22-2 Working drawing. The scale is about 1 grid square to 1/4 inch.

2 Put on your thick leather work gloves, then take the clean can and the V-opener, and work around the bottom-side of the can, punching out the V-shaped holes; best have holes at 3 o'clock, 6 o'clock, 9 o'clock and 12 o'clock and then work more holes in between (FIG. 22-3 left).

3 When you come to cutting the holes around the rim, roll the can opener down-around-and-up, so that the sharp edges are tucked away on the inside of the rim (FIG. 22-3 right).

4 Take the wire, bend the ends around-and-down so as to make an upside down ''U,'' then use the pliers to bend the wire ends through opposite rim holes and back around themselves (FIG. 22-4 left).

5 When you have made the wire handle, give the outside of the can a couple of coats of matte black paint.

6 Finally, when the paint is dry, dribble a pool of glue into the bottom of the can, and then use the two forks to carefully lower the night light into position (FIG. 22-4 right).

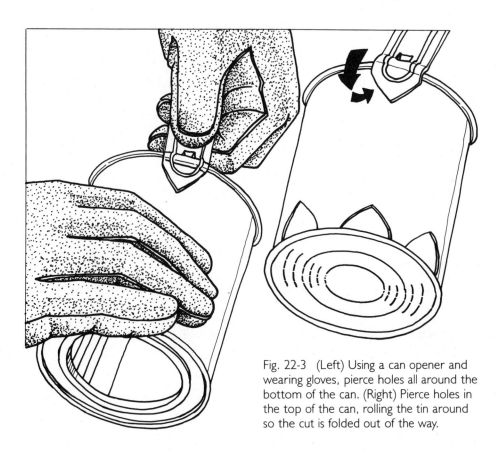

Fig. 22-3 (Left) Using a can opener and wearing gloves, pierce holes all around the bottom of the can. (Right) Pierce holes in the top of the can, rolling the tin around so the cut is folded out of the way.

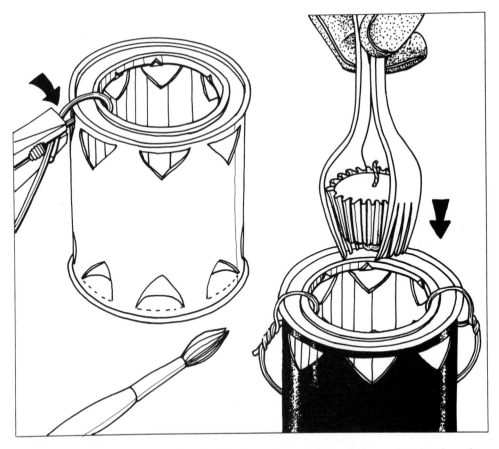

Fig. 22-4 (Left) Thread the wire handle through one of the holes and twist the wire together, using a pair of pliers. (Right) Use two forks to hold the candle, stuck into its case, into the base of the can. Make sure a generous blob of glue is on the foil base of the candle so that it sticks firmly inside the can.

WATCH-POINTS AND FOLLOW-UPS

○ You must wear strong leather work gloves—by work gloves, we mean strong protective gloves

○ When you come to use the lantern, best hang it up or stand it on a fireproof mat. Always ask an adult to check that all is correct, and to light the candle.

Pony Picture

A traditional pin-the-tail-on-the-pony party game

If you have got a party coming up, say a birthday party or maybe a holiday party, then you have just got to play that wonderful old party game—pin-the-tail-on-the-pony. It's really good fun. You hang a picture of a pony up on the wall, and then you blindfold a player and give him a tail with a pin in the end. The object of the game is for the blindfolded player to stick the tail on the correct part of the pony. Of course the good-fun bit—the bit that sets everyone off rolling about and laughing—is watching the poor old player pin-sticking the tail on just about everything except the pony's behind.

Our easy-to-make pony-and-tail game will be a sure-fire winner. Pin it on the wall, blindfold mom or, better still, grandma, and then stand back and watch the fun. What a laugh—a pony with a tail stuck on its nose or on its belly!

MAKING TIME AND SKILL LEVEL

This is perhaps one of the easiest projects in the book, a sheet of paper and a minute or two spent snipping away with a pair of scissors—what could be easier! I would say that, with a little bit of help, an average 7-year-old would be able to make this project in about 5 to 15 minutes.

Cautions and adult help   If you can use a pair of scissors, then the actual making stages are easy. Practice with a pair of scissors and a couple of sheets of newspaper.

Be warned   When the game is being played, you do have to watch out for the pin. If you have any worries at all about the dangers of playing with a stick-pin tail, you could leave out the pin and use a piece of sticky contact putty of the type used in schools for sticking paper to the wall.

TOOLS AND MATERIALS

☐ A sheet of colored paper at about 6×10 inches
☐ A sheet of tracing paper to fit the colored paper
☐ A sheet of dark colored card at about 6×10 inches; it must contrast with the colored paper
☐ A quantity of paper adhesive   ☐ A roll of sticky tape

Continued

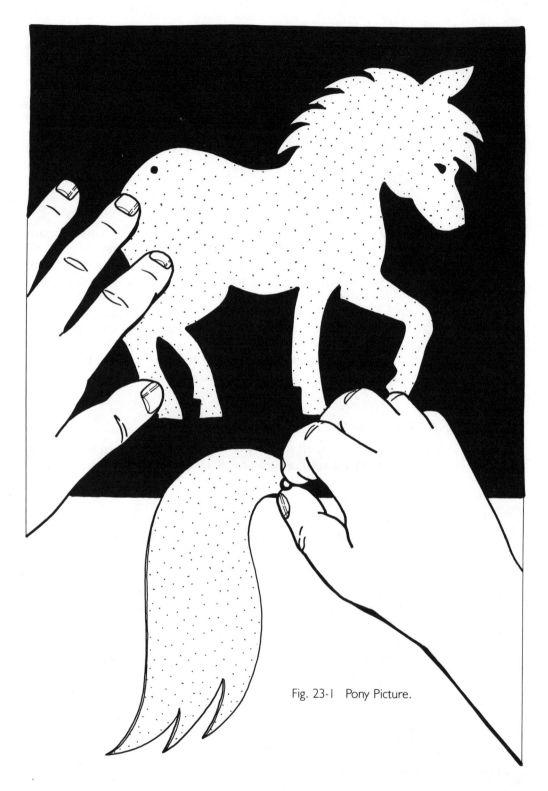

Fig. 23-1 Pony Picture.

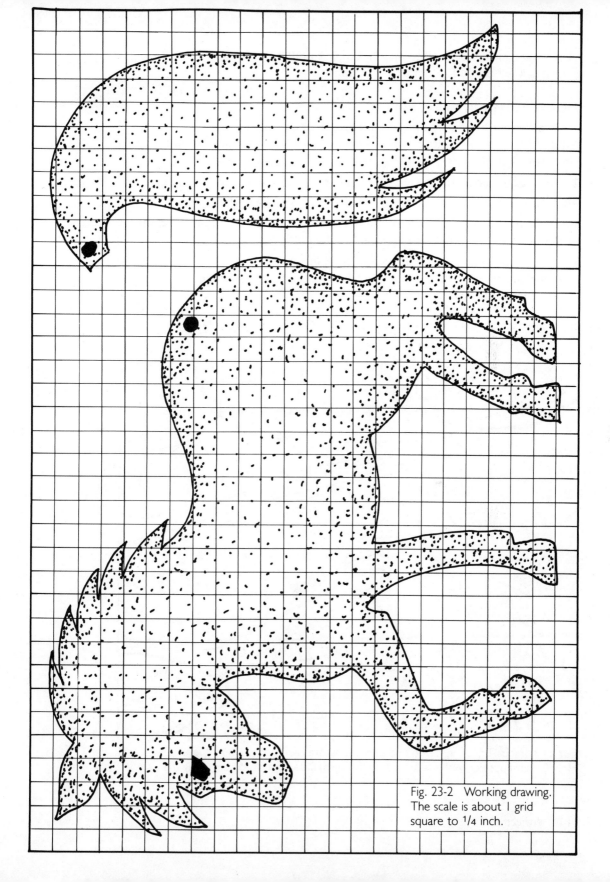

Fig. 23-2 Working drawing.
The scale is about 1 grid
square to 1/4 inch.

☐ A ball-headed dressmaking/map pin ☐ A pencil and ruler
☐ A black felt-tip pen ☐ A pair of scissors

MEASURE, MARK AND MAKE

1 First have a look at the project picture (FIG. 23-1) and the pattern (FIG. 23-2). Note how the pony cutout needs to contrast with the card background, and see also how the pin is fixed to the tail with a small scrap of sticky tape.

2 Having studied all the details, take the pencil and tracing paper, and begin tracing off the two shapes that go to make up the project—the pony and the tail.

3 With the tracing paper held secure with tabs of sticky tape, pencil-press-transfer the traced lines through to best face of the colored paper (FIG. 23-3 top).

4 When you come to the cutting out the pony shape, first swiftly cut away the main lumps of waste. Then, cutting in from the side, slice away the smaller pieces of waste from the main outline (FIG. 23-3 bottom).   *Continued*

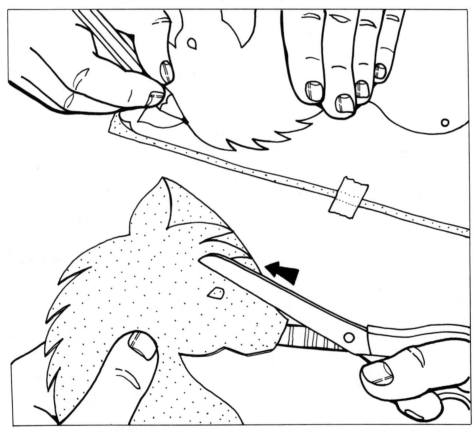

Fig. 23-3 (Top) Trace the design and pencil-press-transfer it through to the colored paper. Hold firmly in position with masking tape. (Bottom) Slice inwards, cutting away the awkward places.

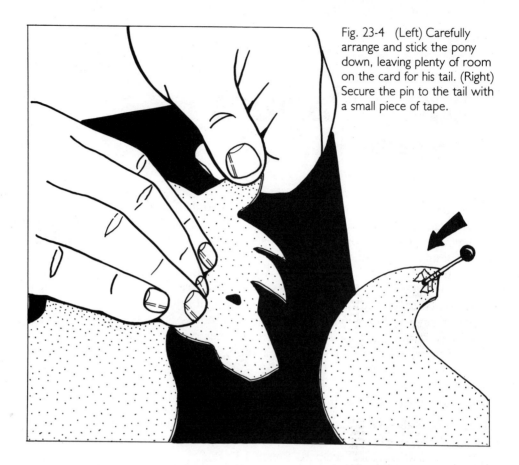

Fig. 23-4 (Left) Carefully arrange and stick the pony down, leaving plenty of room on the card for his tail. (Right) Secure the pin to the tail with a small piece of tape.

5 Smear a thin layer of adhesive over the back of the pony, then carefully arrange and stick the cutout down on the card. Make sure that there is plenty of room left for the tail (FIG. 23-4 left).

6 Finally, spike the pin through the top end of the tail and secure it with a small tab of sticky tape (FIG. 23-4 right).

WATCH-POINTS AND FOLLOW-UPS

○ If you know about grid-square enlarging, or it you can get to use a photocopying machine, you could enlarge our design and make a much larger pony

○ If you like the overall idea of the project, but are not so keen on ponies, you could make a game with a clown-and-nose, or an elephant and a trunk, or . . .

○ If you mount the pony on, say, the back of a tin tray, you could update the project by having the tail stuck onto a magnet.

24

Party Papers
Party garlands

Birthday parties, Christmas parties, parties for adults, and parties for kids—they are all great fun. Music, dancing, singing, playing games, and eating—I'm sure we all like party times. Of course, most of us like the eating bit best, but next in line, I like making the decorations.

Our party garlands are beautiful. A roll of colored crepe paper, a little snip here and a little snip there, and before you can say WOW! you have an amazingly clever party garland decoration. Okay, so you might say that if you have seen one paper decoration then you have seen them all, but it's not so! Our party garland is extra-special and quite unusual because it comes out of the roll ready-twisted, ready-looped, and finished. If you are looking for an instant easy-to-do project, then this is the one for you. It's magic!

MAKING TIME AND SKILL LEVEL

This could well be the easiest project in the book. A few inches a crepe paper sliced off end of the roll, two bits of sticky tape, a quick snip with a pair of scissors, and the project is three-parts finished.

I would say a 6- to 12-year-old could make this project from start to finish in about 3 minutes flat.

Cautions and adult help   Easy and safe, but ever so slightly tricky. Have a few try-outs with a little roll of scrap paper just to see how it goes. As for needing adult help, if you know how to use a pair of scissors, then I think you will be okay.

TOOLS AND MATERIALS

☐ A roll of crepe paper   ☐ A roll of sticky tape   ☐ A pair of scissors

MEASURE, MARK AND MAKE

1   Have a look at the project picture (FIG. 24-1) and the working drawings (FIG. 24-2) and see how the project is easy to make.

2   Roll the crepe paper into a tidy tube shape, mark it off every 3 inches, and see to it that every 3 inch step-off is fixed with two tabs of sticky tape (FIG. 24-3 top).

3   Cut the measured, marked, and tape-fixed crepe paper into 3-inch lengths.

Continued

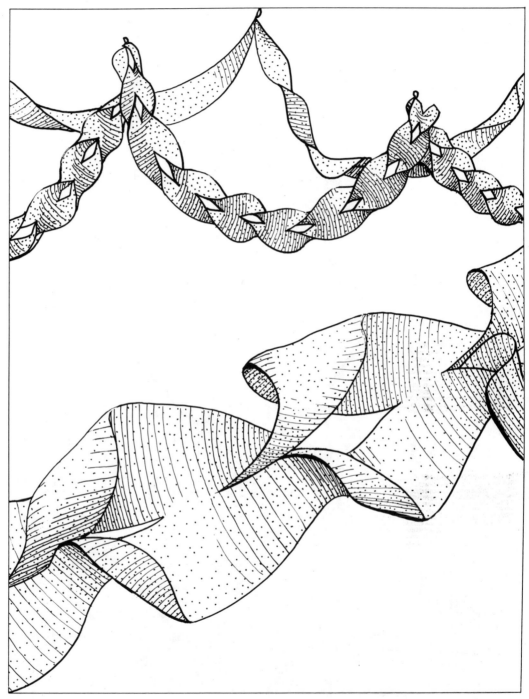

Fig. 24-1 Party Papers.

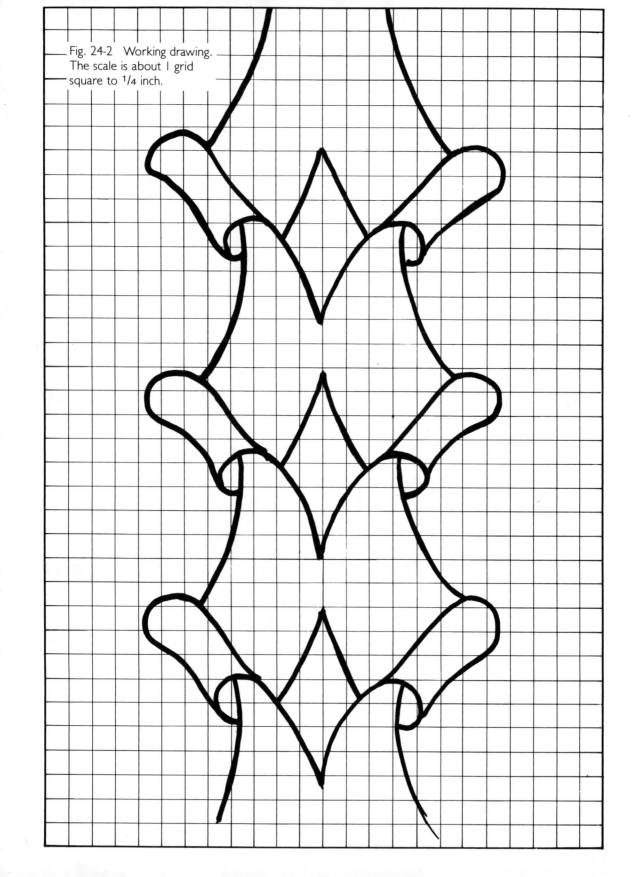

Fig. 24-2 Working drawing.
The scale is about 1 grid
square to 1/4 inch.

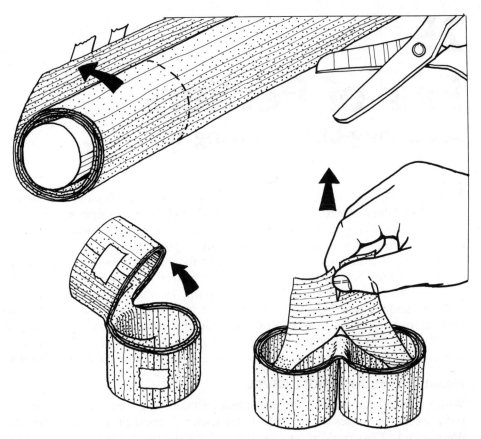

Fig. 24-3 (Top Left) Roll the crepe paper into a long tube shape and mark off every 3 inches. Put tape on to stop it coming undone. Cut the length into 3-inch parts. (Bottom Left) Take each 3-inch piece and make a cut that doesn't quite sever it halfway along its length and fold it back. (Bottom Right) Pull the crepe from the center so that it "folds itself" into a beautiful chain.

4 Take a 3-inch tube and make a mark 1$^{1}/_{2}$ inches along its length.

5 Cut the crepe tube through the halfway mark. Make sure that the cut only goes about three-quarters of the way through the tube thickness (FIG. 24-3 bottom left).

6 With the two half-tubes still linked and sitting end-down on the worksurface, take hold of the inside-center end, and slowly draw it up and out so as to make the linked and twisted chain (FIG. 24-3 bottom).

WATCH-POINTS AND FOLLOW-UPS

○ Make sure that the roll of crepe paper is fixed with the tabs of sticky tape.
○ If you have any doubts as to how to work the project, make a try-out with a sheet of scrap paper.

25
Pair of Peckers
A pecking-birds moving toy

Our pecking birds toy is really good fun. Hold the two handles and pull them in and out, and the two birds start to peck up seed. Peck peck, peck peck, you would think that the birds might miss a peck or two and start to peck each other, but it never happens. Peck peck, peck peck—they happily bob backwards and forwards, turn, and turn about. Simple four-pivot mechanical toys of this type come in many shapes and forms: there are little boxers who take turns throwing punches, there are men with swords, and so on. They are sometimes known as "Muzhik and the Bear" type toys, because the most popular toy shows a Russian peasant, or *muzhik,* and a bear sitting on a log and taking turns chopping wood.

If you would like to make a traditional Russian folk toy, say, as a present for a friend or maybe even as a desk-toy for your dad, then this is the project for you.

MAKING TIME AND SKILL LEVEL

With this particular project, the measuring and cutting are easy enough, but the putting-together stages are just a little bit tricky. A good project for older children—a 9- to 12-year-old should be able to have the toy made in about 20 to 30 minutes.

Cautions and adult help   Although you should be able to manage most of this project on your own, best ask for help when you come to the putting together stages. Watch out that you don't mixup the various pivot holes.

Be warned   No real problems with this project, just watch out for the scissors, and be careful that you don't lose the little brass tab clips.

TOOLS AND MATERIALS

☐ A quantity of cardboard; best to have thick card for the four strips and a slightly thinner card for the two birds.
☐ A sheet of tracing paper   ☐ A pencil and ruler   ☐ A pair of scissors
☐ A wooden block and a large nail   ☐ A hammer
☐ A packet of colored felt-tip pens   ☐ Four brass fold-tab paper clips

MEASURE, MARK AND MAKE

1   Study the project picture (FIG. 25-1) and the working drawings (FIG. 25-2), and see how the toy is made and put together. Note how the two birds are sandwiched between four cardboard strips and how they are set facing each other.

Continued

Fig. 25-1   A Pair of Peckers.

2 Trace off the design and carefully pencil-press-transfer the traced lines through to the various pieces of card. Make sure that the holes are all correctly placed (FIG. 25-3, top left).

3 Cut out the four identical cardboard strips (FIG. 25-3 bottom).

4 One piece at a time, support the strips on the wooden block and punch out the pivot holes with the hammer and nail. Each strip needs to have two carefully placed holes (FIG. 25-3 top right).

5 Use the felt-tip pens to color in the birds and the strips. Go for delicate pale pastel colors like blue, pink, yellow, and green (FIG. 25-4 top).

Continued

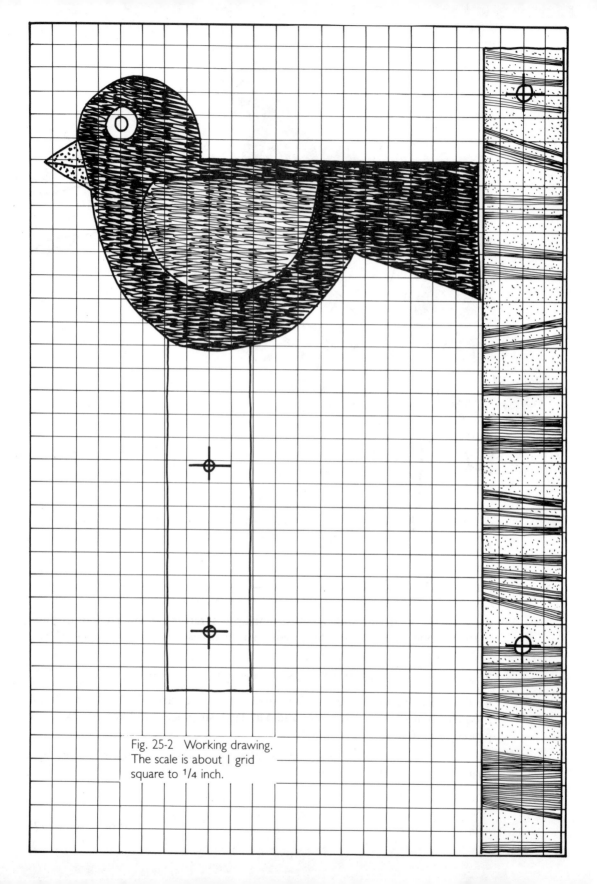

Fig. 25-2 Working drawing.
The scale is about 1 grid
square to 1/4 inch.

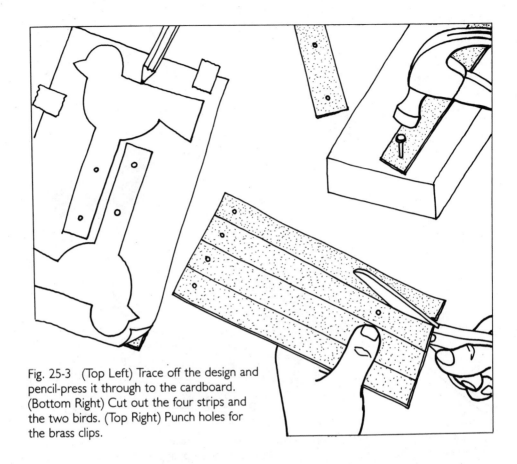

Fig. 25-3 (Top Left) Trace off the design and pencil-press it through to the cardboard. (Bottom Right) Cut out the four strips and the two birds. (Top Right) Punch holes for the brass clips.

6 Finally, set the four strips together so that the bird's legs are sandwiched. Make sure that all the holes are aligned and then fit-and-fix the various layers with the four brass fold-tab clips (FIG. 25-4 bottom).

WATCH-POINTS AND FOLLOW-UPS

○ If you want to take this project a little further, you could use this project as a cardboard prototype (see Glossary), then you could go on to make the toy in wood by tracing the picture on 1/8-inch-thick multicore plywood.

○ If you have put the toy together carefully, the strips should be parallel to each other.

Fig. 25-4 (Top Left) Use felt-tip pens to color in the pieces. Face the birds beak to beak, so the color is correct on both sides. (Bottom Right) Use the strips in pairs and sandwich the legs of the birds between them. Use brass clips in the holes to secure them.

Mad Monkey
A traditional Victorian counterbalance toy

We all like monkeys! Monkeys jumping and swinging from trees, monkeys in zoos, monkeys in cartoons, and monkeys on the TV—with their cheeky faces, large ears, beautiful eyes, and long tails, monkeys are great fun. I wonder why monkeys are so popular? Do you think that it has anything to do with the fact that they remind us of each other!

But anyway, our Mad Monkey is extra special. Would you believe he can balance on almost anything? He can balance on a taut wire or on the rim of a bowl or on the edge of a shelf or cup. He's a pretty cool customer. As to why our monkey is so clever, ask your parents and your teachers, and see what they have to say. Mention the key word "counterbalance."

You could make whole families of monkeys. Long-tailed monkeys, chimps, wooly monkeys—you could have them balanced on a line across your bedroom.

MAKING TIME AND SKILL LEVEL

No problem with this project, a scrap or two of thick card, 10 minutes or so with a pair of scissors and before you can say "Cheetah," your monkey will be finished. Okay, so you might find the card-cutting a bit difficult; best to practice first with some odd pieces of cardboard. Experiment with a breakfast cereal box. See if you can cut out the letters and some part of the design.

Cautions and adult help   If you are a beginner or if you haven't used a pair of scissors before, ask an adult to show you how.

If, after trying, you can't cut along a drawn line, or if you find the scissors difficult to manage or the card too thick to cut, ask an adult to help you out.

Be warned   Sharp-pointed scissors can be dangerous. Watch out for your eyes, and be extra careful when younger brothers and sisters are about.

TOOLS AND MATERIALS

☐ A piece of thick cardboard about 7×4 inches; best if the card is white.
☐ A pencil and ruler   ☐ A sheet of tracing paper at 7×4 inches
☐ A pair of scissors   ☐ Acrylic paints in the colors orange and black
☐ A couple of small brushes, one broad and the other fine-point

Continued

☐ Four small white circles of waste from a paper punch; you could use lick-and-stick, or press-stick dots
☐ A small amount of paper adhesive

MEASURE, MARK AND MAKE

I Have a look at the project picture (FIG. 26-1) and the working pattern (FIG. 26-2) and see how the monkey needs to be cut from a piece of thick card. See how the long, curved tail acts as a counterbalance.

Continued

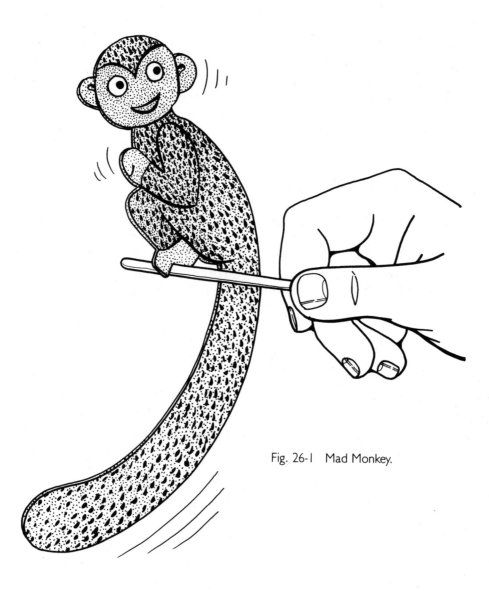

Fig. 26-1 Mad Monkey.

Fig. 26-2 Working drawing. The scale is about 1 grid square to 1/4 inch.

2 When you have studied the various drawings and maybe even made a rough working prototype, then carefully trace off the design and pencil-press-transfer the main outline through to the best face of your chosen piece of card (FIG. 26-3 top).

3 Having made sure that the outline is nice and clear, first use the scissors to cut away the main areas of waste (FIG. 26-3 left) and then carefully follow around the main outline (FIG. 26-3 right).

4 Give the monkey a generous coat of orange acrylic paint; make sure that all the edges and corners are well covered (FIG. 26-4 top left).

5 When the orange paint is dry, take the tracing and pencil-press-transfer the details—the eyes, mouth and the like—through to both sides of the cutout (FIG. 26-4 top right).

6 Use a fine-point brush and the black acrylic paint to pick out all the details.

Continued

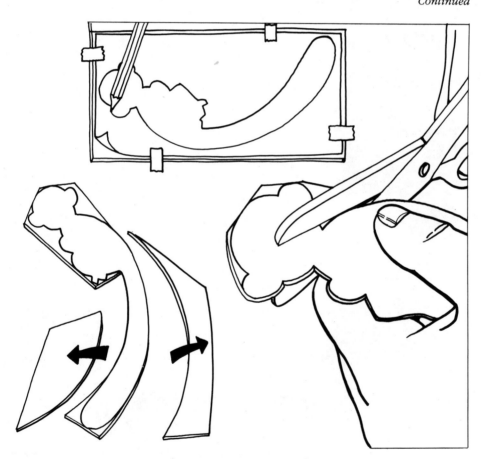

Fig. 26-3 (Top) Trace and transfer the design onto the card. (Bottom Left) Cut unwanted areas from the main shape. (Bottom Right) Cut into and away the smaller unwanted card.

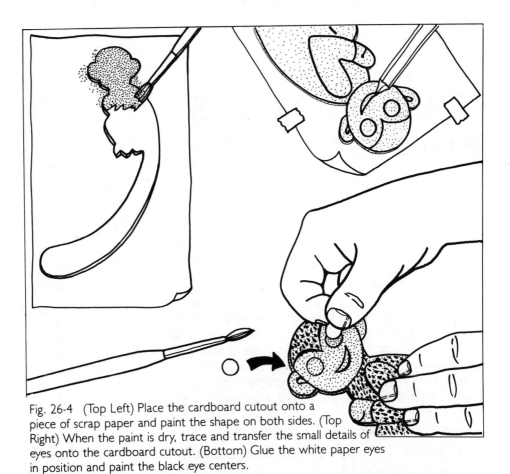

Fig. 26-4 (Top Left) Place the cardboard cutout onto a piece of scrap paper and paint the shape on both sides. (Top Right) When the paint is dry, trace and transfer the small details of eyes onto the cardboard cutout. (Bottom) Glue the white paper eyes in position and paint the black eye centers.

7 Finally, stick on the little white eyes, dab in black eye-dots, and the monkey is ready for the fun (FIG. 26-4 bottom).

WATCH-POINTS AND FOLLOW-UPS

○ If you like the general idea of the project and want to go on to make other animals, sort out the counterbalance problems by experimenting with cardboard and plastercine prototypes.

○ If for some reason your monkey is off-balance, adjust the weight by adding one or more paper clips to the tail.

○ If you decide to improve the design by giving the monkey say little bead-in-bubble type moving eyes or whatever, then be prepared to change the size and the weight of the tail.

27
Wet Weapons
An origami water-bomb

Origami is the Japanese art and craft of folding paper. The word "origami" is made up from two smaller Japanese words, "*ori*" meaning folding, and "*gami*" meaning paper.

You will love our origami water-bomb. It's a great toy; its a real wow! Better still, its very easy to make. A square sheet of paper, a few careful folds, and before you can say "splish-splash," the cube-shaped bomb is finished and ready for action. The best part is filling the bomb up with water and using it in a surprise attack. But who to throw it at? Your dad? Your mom? Your brother or sister? Your sister's boyfriends? Your best friend? You need to do a bit of careful thinking about it. Of course, you can only use it out-of-doors, and, really, you ought to give some advance warning, but that said, an origami water-bomb is a safe, good-fun summertime toy. But don't forget, once the word gets around that you are making water-bombs, you also might be in for a splash or two.

MAKING TIME AND SKILL LEVEL

Japanese origami is very much like, arithmetic, dancing, and living. It's simple when you know how! That said, I would reckon that an 8- to 12-year-old ought to be able to make a bomb in about 5 to 15 minutes.

Cautions and adult help   Practice with a few sheets of scrap newspaper first. You won't need adult help.

Be warned   Don't forget, if you drop a water bomb on, say, your brother, then chances are, you will be next in line for a wet surprise. Best choose a nice sunny day when everyone is dressed in shorts and sweat shirts. *Do not throw water bombs at aged grandparents, babies, or pets.*

TOOLS AND MATERIALS

☐ A square of good-quality paper at about 5 × 5 inches.

MEASURE, MARK AND MAKE

1   Have a look at the project picture (FIG. 27-1) and the working drawing page (FIG. 27-2) and see how the paper is folded to make a watertight cube.

Continued

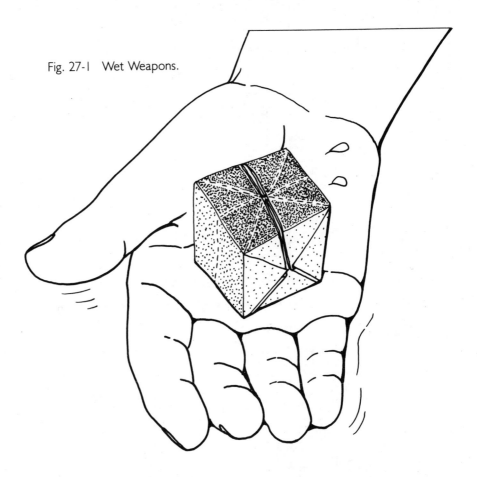

Fig. 27-1 Wet Weapons.

2 When you have had a few practice try-outs, take the square of paper and carefully fold and crease it from corner-to-corner (FIG. 27-3 top left).

3 Turn the folded paper over and fold it from side-to-side (FIG. 27-3 top right).

4 Pinch in the side of the paper square so as to make a triangular cup-like cone (FIG. 27-3 bottom left).

5 With the V-shaped cone flat-down on the table, turn the two corners down to bottom-center to make a little square (FIG. 27-3 bottom right and middle). Do this with both sides.

6 With the square set flat-down, fold the side-corners into the center so as to make a boat shape (FIG. 27-4 top left). Do this with both sides.

7 Fold the small flap in half (FIG. 27-4 top middle). Do this with all four flaps.

8 One side at a time, pinch open the little triangular side pockets and tuck the flaps inside (FIG. 27-4 top right and bottom left).

Continued

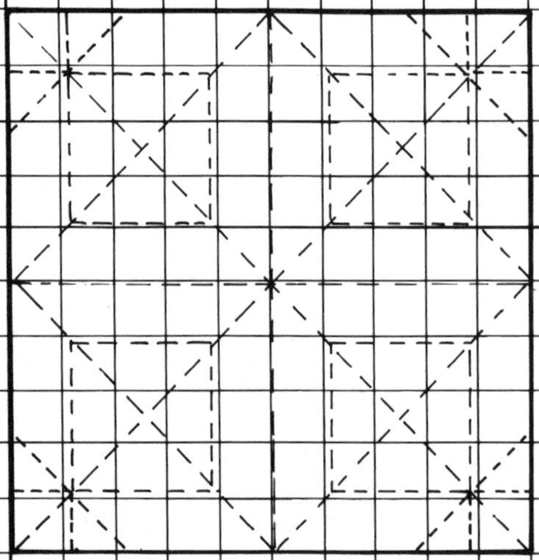

Fig. 27-2 Working drawing.
The scale is about 1 grid
square to 1/2 inch.

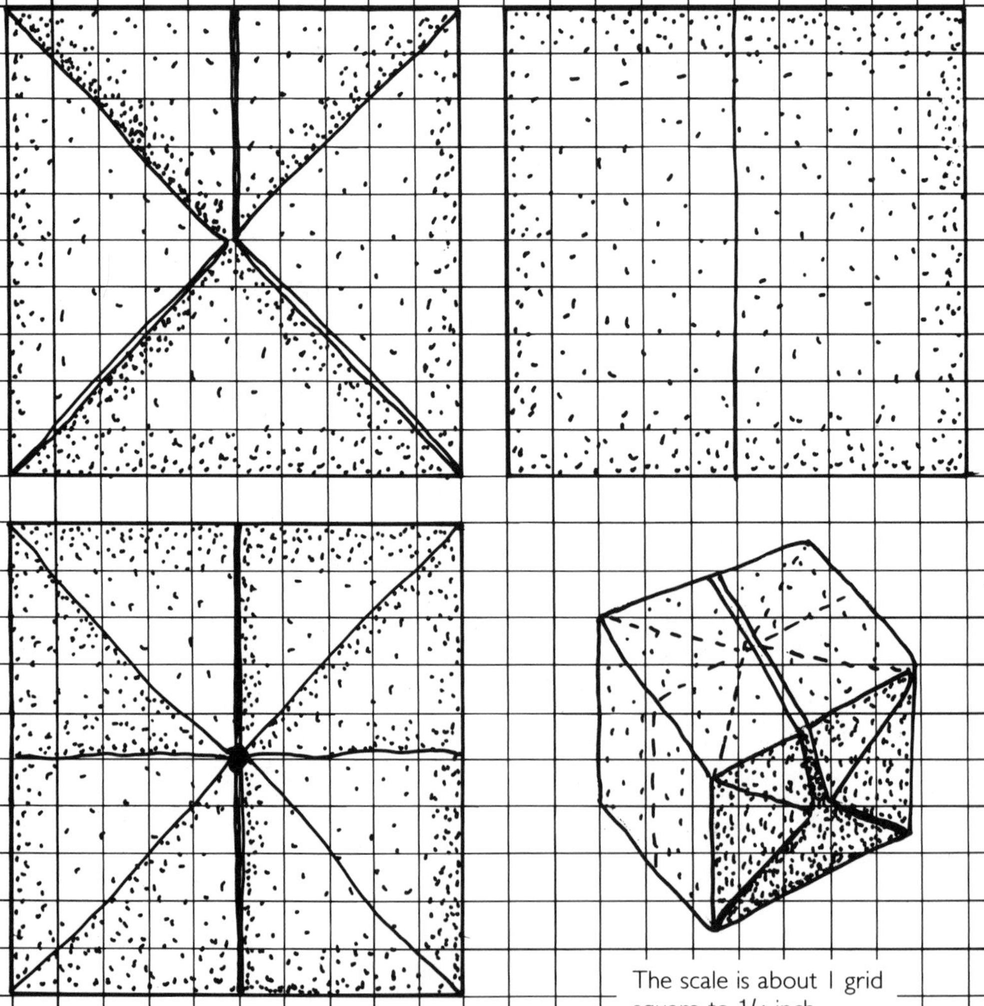

The scale is about 1 grid
square to 1/4 inch.

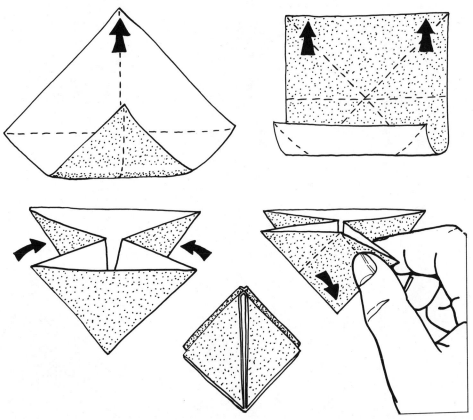

Fig. 27-3 (Top Left) Fold the paper corner to corner to form a cross. (Top Right) Turn the paper over, and fold in half. (Bottom Left) Turn the paper over, and pinch in the sides forming a triangle. (Bottom Right) Fold all four corners down to form a square.

9 Ease the sides out, and blow into the top hole so as to make the little cube shape (FIG. 27-4 bottom middle and right).

10 Finally, fill the paper cube up with clean, cold water and get ready to run.

WATCH-POINTS AND FOLLOW-UPS

○ Use a good-quality typing paper
○ Make sure that your hands are clean and dry, and be careful not to over-crease the folds
○ Water-bombs are fun, but only if all your "victims" really want to join in!

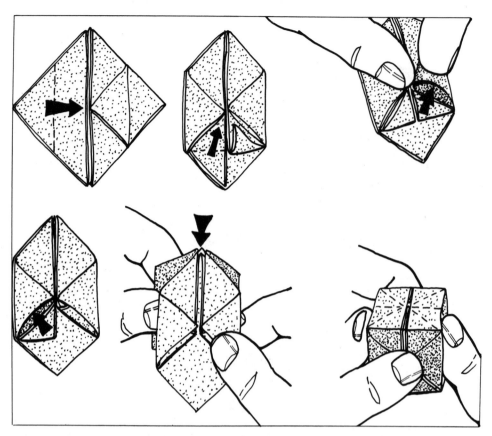

Fig. 27-4 (Top Left) Fold the side corners into the center, do this to both sides to form a boat shape. (Top Middle) Fold the tiny bottom flaps in half—do this with all four. (Top Right) Pinch open the side flaps, forcing the thumb and the other hand in to enlarge the opening. (Bottom Left) Roll the little folded flap into this space, pushing it in and squeezing it flat with your thumb. Do this with all four. (Bottom Middle) Hold the two "sides" and blow into the hole at the top and push the sides in to form a box shape.

Grandma and Grandpa
"Shelf people" dolls

Shelf people are really contented folk. They don't need to go whizzing about in fast cars, nor do they need feeding and constant fussing around like, say, cats and dogs. All they ask is that you sit them on a shelf and let them be. Okay, so some shelf people do prefer to be sitting next to books, while others seem to be happiest sitting high up on the topmost shelf, but that aside, they like a quiet life. You might think that shelf people miss out on things, but it isn't so. They see everything. They see us first thing in the morning and last thing at night. They watch us when we are being naughty. Certainly they don't say much, but my goodness, they know exactly what's going on!

Our grandma and grandpa shelf people are really good fun. Sit them on a shelf in your bedroom and you have got a couple of friends for life.

MAKING TIME AND SKILL LEVEL

Although our shelf people are made of thin plywood, this is not to say that the making stages are in any way complex or difficult. Certainly, you do need to be able to use a coping or fret saw, but that aside, the making stages are pretty straightforward. I would say that a 10- to 12-year-old should be able to get a shelf person made in the space of a morning.

Cautions and adult help Small handsaws are both easy to use and safe—just take it nice and steady. Hold the saw so that the blade runs through the wood at right angles to the working surface and don't try to rush. If you have never used a saw before, decide how you want the project to be, then ask an adult to spend 10 minutes showing you how.

Be warned If you are a beginner, the chances are, you will spend a great deal of time breaking saw blades. Don't worry too much about the blades, because, after all, practice does make perfect. Just make sure that you have a spare pack of blades.

Fig. 28-1 Grandma and Grandpa.

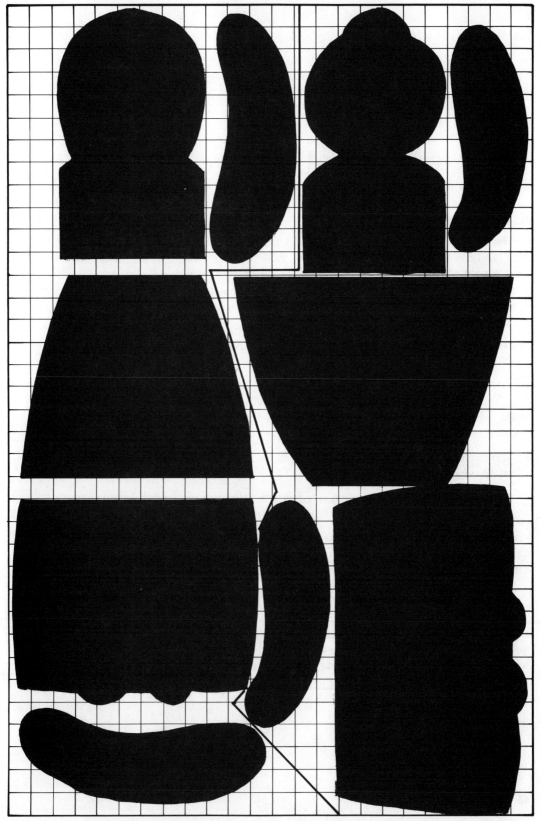

Fig. 28-2 Cutting Plan. The scale is about I grid square to ¹/4 inch.

TOOLS AND MATERIALS

☐ A 6-×-9-inch sheet of 1/4-inch-thick plywood for each shelf person that you want to make.

☐ The use of a workbench with a vise ☐ A pencil and ruler

☐ A sheet of tracing paper ☐ A coping or fret saw

☐ A pack of graded sandpapers

☐ A small tube/container of white PVA wood glue

☐ A handful of small panel pins ☐ A small hammer

☐ A selection of broad and fine-point paint brushes

☐ A good selection of acrylic paints

MEASURE, MARK AND MAKE

I Have a good long look at the project picture (FIG. 28-1), the cutting plan (FIG. 28-2), and the two working drawings (FIG. 28-3 and FIG. 28-4), and see how each shelf person is made up from five pieces of 1/4-inch-thick plywood. Note how the three main cutouts are glued and pinned at right angles to each other, and see also how the arms are fitted and fixed from the shoulders through to the lap.

2 Trace off the designs and pencil-press-transfer the traced lines through to the working face of the plywood. You need five shapes for each figure a head-and-shoulders, a lap or waist-to-knees, a knees-to-toes, and two arms (FIG. 28-5 top left).

3 Clamp the wood in the vise and set to it with the coping saw. Keep to the waste side of the drawn lines and aim for cuts that are clean and crisp (FIG. 28-5 bottom right).

4 When you have cut out the various pieces, take the graded sandpapers and rub down all the sharp burrs and jags.

5 Note which way around the two edge-to-side joints are set, and then put them together with the PVA glue and the panel pins (FIG. 28-6 left).

6 To fit the two arms, first glue and pin them through to the shoulders (FIG. 28-6 top), then swing the hands down until they are touching the knees and fix them with a dab of glue.

7 Use the graded sandpapers to rub down all the sharp edges and corners. Aim for a smooth, slightly round-edged finish.

8 When you come to painting on the acrylic colors, first lay on the main ground coats, and then, when the paint is dry, pick out the details with a fine-point brush. Best go for bold primary colors (red, blue, yellow) with the details picked out in fine black lines (FIG. 28-6 bottom right).

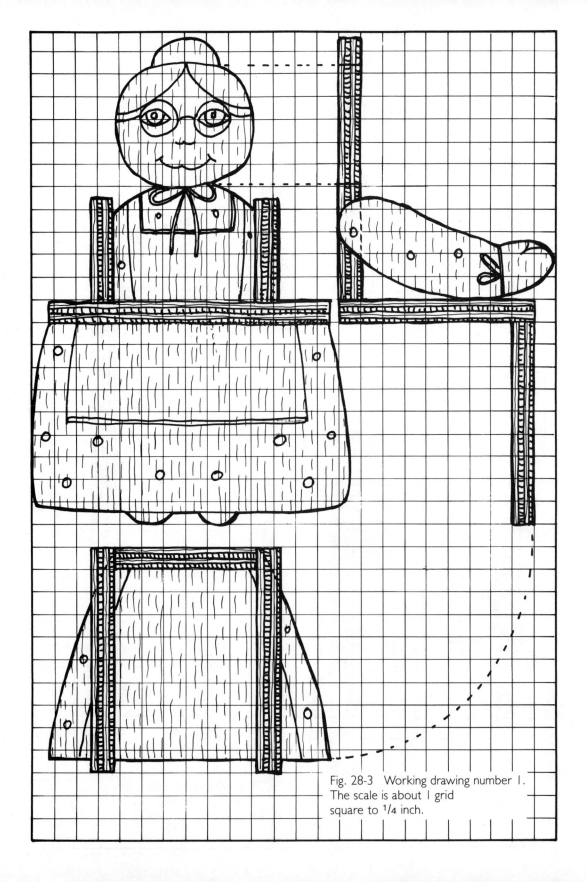

Fig. 28-3 Working drawing number 1.
The scale is about 1 grid
square to 1/4 inch.

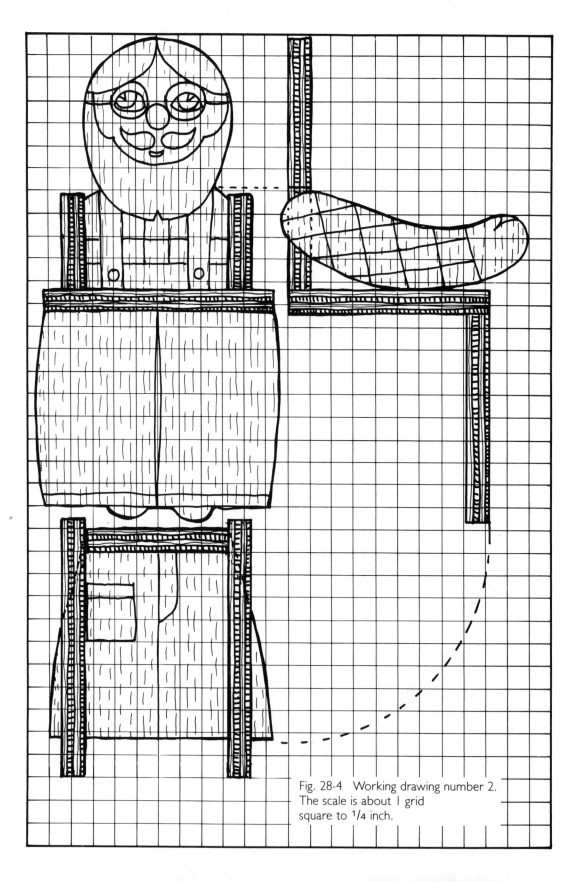

Fig. 28-4 Working drawing number 2.
The scale is about 1 grid
square to 1/4 inch.

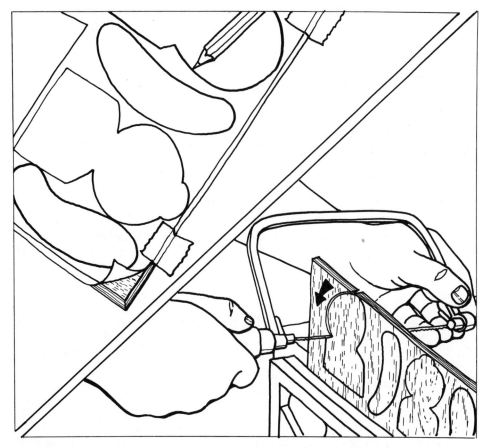

Fig. 28-5 (Top Left) Pencil-press-transfer the lines of the design onto the wood. (Bottom Right) Turn the blade to face the line of the design, and saw on the outside of that line.

WATCH-POINTS AND FOLLOW-UPS

○ If you like the project, but don't much like the idea of working in wood, you could use thick cardboard.

○ When you are choosing your plywood, go for a smooth, white-faced, multi-core ply, the type of plywood that has lots of thin layers.

○ When you are nailing through the joints, best support the wood on a block of wood; ask an adult to give you a hand.

○ Although PVA glue makes a good solid joint, you could speed things up by using a hot glue gun or contact adhesive.

Fig. 28-6 (Left) Use a block of wood to support the pieces of the figure during assembly. Glue and pin each piece into place. (Right) Paint the large areas of the figures—that is, all the "background." Then use a fine brush to paint the detail of the face and dress.

29

Grisly Greetings
A pop-up greeting card

We all like receiving greeting cards. To come down in the morning and open a whole stack of cards wishing us well—it's a really good feeling. But our greeting card is a card with a difference; it's phantasmagorically, fantastically fearsome. Our "Grisly Bear" greeting card is a real horror. When you open and close the card, the bear opens and closes his mouth. Just wait until your friends open the card and the pop-open jaws of the bear gape to reveal a large set of teeth. Your friends will be amazed, surprised, and altogether horrified. Only joking, of course; our grisly bear, or perhaps I should say grizzly bear, is, in fact, a friendly sort of pal.

If you are looking to make a really good greeting card, a card that's a little bit special and unusual, then this is the project for you. Grisly Grizzly is great fun!

MAKING TIME AND SKILL LEVEL

This is a pretty straightforward project. A bit of tracing and cutting, a snip or two with the scissors and the job is done. I would say most 6- to 12-year-olds could make the card in about 20 to 30 minutes.

Cautions and adult help   Perhaps the sticking down of the mouth is a little bit tricky. Practice first with a bit of scrap paper, and then ask for help if you need it.

Be warned   No problems or warnings with this project; it's safe and it's easy!

TOOLS AND MATERIALS

☐ A sheet of thin, smooth cardboard about 6×9 inches. Best if it's a light pastel color like pale brown or cream.
☐ A sheet of tracing paper to fit the card   ☐ A few scraps of white paper
☐ A pencil and ruler   ☐ A glue stick
☐ A pack of colored pencil crayons to include the colors red/orange, brown, and black.

MEASURE, MARK AND MAKE

1   First have a look at the project picture (FIG. 29-1) and the working drawing (FIG. 29-2), and see how the bear needs to be drawn out so that it fits into the fold of the card. See also how the small disk of white paper is folded, cut, and mounted over the bear's face to make the pop-up muzzle.

Continued

Fig. 29-1 Grisly Greetings.

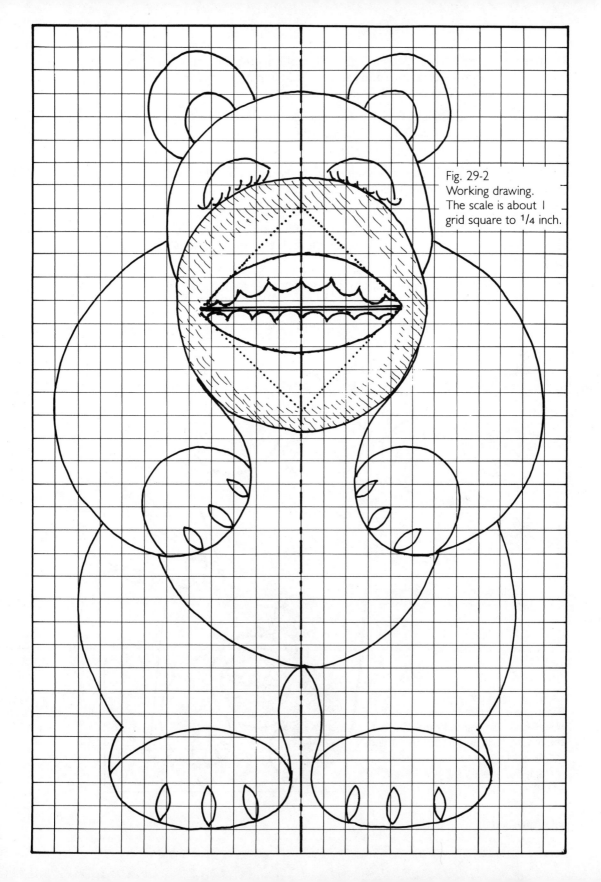

Fig. 29-2
Working drawing.
The scale is about 1
grid square to 1/4 inch.

2 When you have a good, clear understanding of how the project is put together, take the 6-x-9-inch sheet of card and carefully fold it in half longways, so that you have a book-fold that measures 3×9 inches (FIG. 19-1).

3 Trace off the design and pencil-press-transfer the traced lines through to the inside face of the folded card. Make sure that the toes-to-nose center-line matches up with the fold (FIG. 29-3 top).

4 Use the pencil crayons to color in the bear. Make a dark brown/black outline of the bear, then color the ears, head, arms, and legs brown and the ears and mouth red. Leave the eyelids, paws, and tummy the natural card color (FIG. 29-3 bottom).

5 Trace off the total front-face muzzle area. Then pencil-press-transfer the traced lines through to the white card. Cut out the muzzle area; it should be almost round.

6 Fold the round shape in half along the center nose-to-chin line, and cut the mouth slot (FIG. 29-4 left).

7 Carefully fold the four circle quarters in towards the center of the circle to make the fold lines (FIG. 29-4 top).

Continued

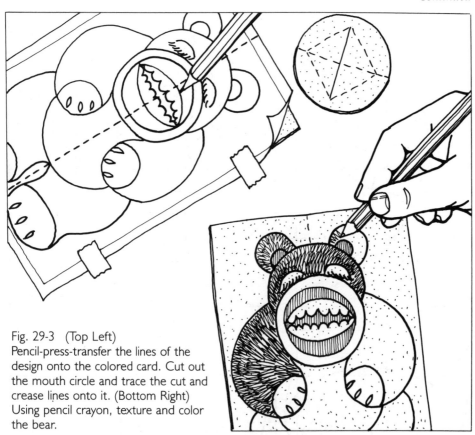

Fig. 29-3 (Top Left)
Pencil-press-transfer the lines of the design onto the colored card. Cut out the mouth circle and trace the cut and crease lines onto it. (Bottom Right) Using pencil crayon, texture and color the bear.

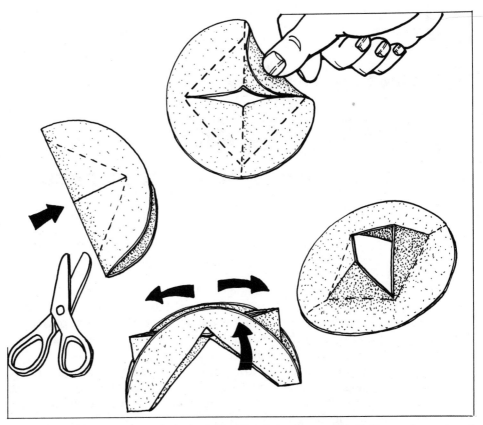

Fig. 29-4 (Left) Cut the mouth slot by folding the circle of paper in half. Crease the center of the four fold lines, forming a square within the circle. (Bottom Left) Pull the "mouth" open and fold the circle in half, shutting the mouth inside. Crease the two fold lines with your thumb. Open up the shape and it is ready to glue on the card.

8 Crease the fold lines, and fold the circle in half so that the mouth is open and inside the fold. If all is correct, the mouth should be open when the circle is folded and closed when the circle is opened out (FIG. 29-4 bottom left).

9 Finally, open the circle flat-out, and glue it in place on the bear's face. Make sure that the nose-to-chin center-line of the circle is lined up with the center-line fold of the card (FIG. 29-4 bottom right).

WATCH-POINTS AND FOLLOW-UPS

○ If you like the idea of the pop-up mouth, but don't much like the bear, then you could change the design and make a large bird or a frog or whatever. You could also have the card folded from side to side, or make two pop-up frog's eyes.

○ The muzzle disk is a little bit tricky. Best to practice first with a bit of scrap card.

○ If you decide to make a bigger card, make sure that you can get an envelope to fit.

Grisly Greetings 151

30

Sammy the Surprise Spider

A Christmas piñata or sweet surprise

Known variously around the world as Christmas Surprises, Christmas Treats, and, in Mexico, as Christmas Piñatas, the piñata is a large, hollow, decorative paper form full of sweets, treats, and little presents. At Christmastime the piñata is hung from the ceiling and then the fun begins. One at a time, children are blindfolded and given a rolled up newspaper. The object of the game is to lash out with the newspaper so as to break the hanging shape. Of course, when the piñata is at last broken, all the children are showered with goodies. As you can imagine, half the fun is watching the children having near misses.

Our Sammy Surprise Spider is a wonderful piñata. With his beautiful round body, he's just asking to be swatted. Hang him up at Christmastime, or at just about any other time of the year, and he will make sure that your celebration goes with a bang and a swing. It's good fun!

MAKING TIME AND SKILL LEVEL

Making Sammy the Spider is a lengthy business, but only because he needs to be made over several days. I would say a 6- to 12-year-old could have this project made in about three evenings.

Cautions and adult help   Covering the balloon is a bit tricky. Best work as an adult-child team.

Be warned   If you are rough with the balloon, it might go BANG!

TOOLS AND MATERIALS

- ☐ A large balloon; best to buy a whole packet just in case
- ☐ A supply of old newspapers   ☐ A packet of wallpaper paste/adhesive
- ☐ A brush   ☐ Several packets of small sweets, treats, and party favors
- ☐ A can of black acrylic paint   ☐ A ball of strong knitting yarn
- ☐ A few large sheets of colored tissue paper   ☐ A large bodkin needle
- ☐ A pair of scissors   ☐ A roll of sticky tape

MEASURE, MARK AND MAKE

1 Have a look at the project picture (FIG. 30-1) and the working drawing page (FIG. 30-2) and see how the spider is made and put together. Note the way the body is made from thin strips of torn newspaper, and see also how the strips of zigzag tissue are threaded on the yarn to make up the spider's eight legs.

Continued

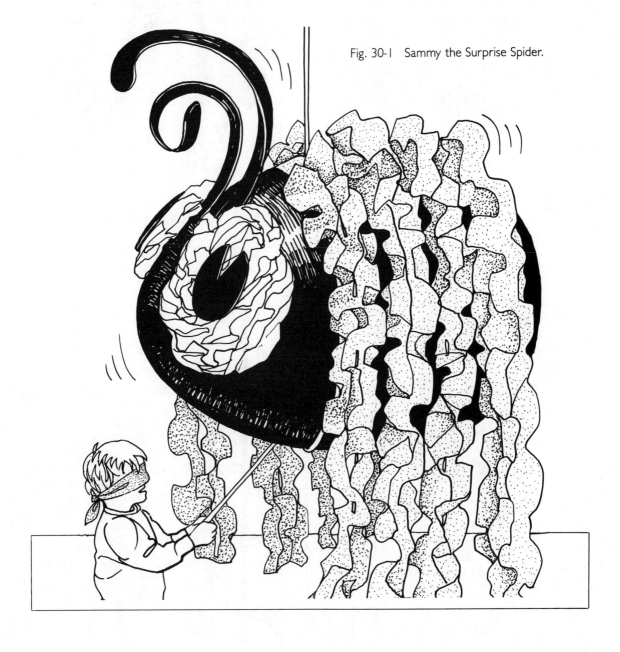

Fig. 30-1 Sammy the Surprise Spider.

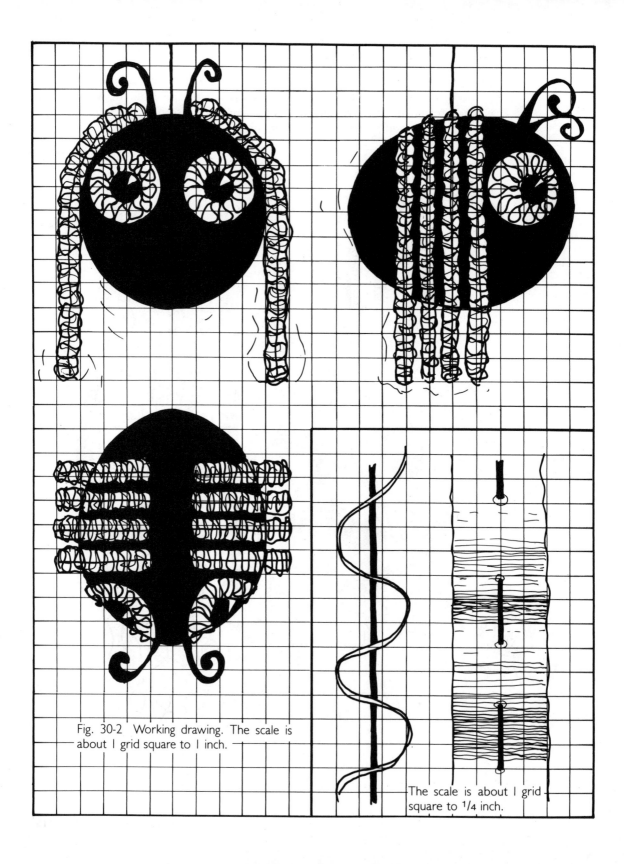

Fig. 30-2 Working drawing. The scale is about I grid square to I inch.

The scale is about I grid square to $1/4$ inch.

2   Tear the newspaper into narrow strips. Soak each strip with glue, and then, one strip at a time, start to cover the balloon (FIG. 30-3 top left).

3   Remembering to leave a small uncovered area around the mouthpiece, gradually work backwards and forwards over the balloon until the paper covering is at least three strips thick.

4   When the paper is dry and the shape is hard and firm, cut off the mouthpiece, remove the balloon, and fill the balloon-shaped shell with sweets (FIG. 30-3 top right).

5   Use glued strips of newspaper to carefully patch the hole (FIG. 30-3 bottom left).

Continued

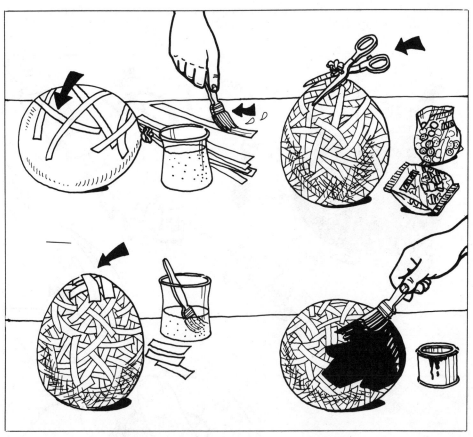

Fig. 30-3   (Top Left) Using a wide brush, saturate each strip of newspaper with glue. Then brush each strip over onto the surface of the balloon. Note: Leave the top of the balloon uncovered. (Top Right) When it is dry, cut the "nozzle" and the balloon will deflate. Remove the balloon, and fill the "shell/body" with sweets. (Bottom Left) Using newspaper strips and glue, cover the hole and leave to dry. (Bottom Right) Paint the "body" black.

Sammy the Surprise Spider   155

6 When the patch is completely dry, give the whole shell a thick, generous coat of black acrylic paint (FIG. 30-3 bottom right).

7 Cut the tissue paper into 2-inch-wide strips. You need 16 strips in all, two for each leg.

8 Take two strips of tissue paper and thread them up on the yarn. Fix the leg ends with tabs of sticky tape and have two legs threaded up on each yarn length (FIG. 30-4 middle).

9 Take the gathered-tissue legs and ease the tissue apart to make the full fluffy effect (FIG. 30-4 bottom right).

10 Finally, when you come to putting the spider together, fit-and-fix the paired legs over the body so that they hang down each side. Loop the "hanging" string right around the body and fix it with a sticky-tape patch. Use balled up tissue and cut paper for the eyes, and make the two antennae from strips of coiled black paper (FIG. 30-4 top left).

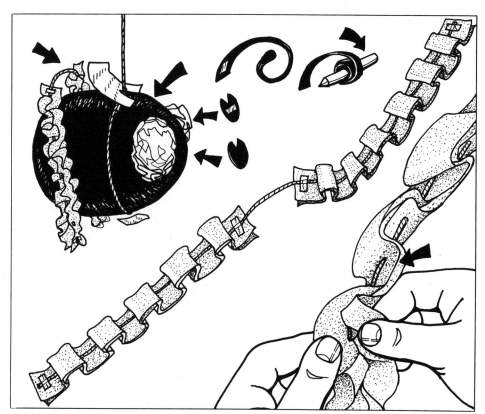

Fig. 30-4 (Top Left) Adding the details to the spider, the legs, the antennae, and the eyes. Secure all with tape; use strong parcel tape to hold the suspension cord in place, as this has to be strong to withstand many whacks. (Middle and Bottom) Gather and tape the tissue strips for the legs. Open out and separate the tissue before attaching it to the spider body.

WATCH-POINTS AND FOLLOW-UPS

○ Make sure that you use a water-based paste or glue for gluing the newspaper strips.

○ Be warned: if you dry the paper-covered shape too fast, the balloon might burst; best dry it out slowly.

○ If you like the idea of the project, but are not so keen on spiders, you could make a pig, a Santa Claus, a spaceship, a monster's head, or just about any design that strikes your fancy.

○ If you get the tissue paper wet, it's likely the color will run. Best fix the legs with tabs of sticky tape.

○ Because the poor old spider needs to stand up to quite a few whacks, make sure that the "hanging" cord is strong and that the around-body loop is well fixed with tabs of sticky tape.

31
Off with a Bang
A whizz-bang party noisemaker

Whizz-Bangers are noisy; whizz-bangers are thunder-makers; whizz-bangers are the perfect lift for a rainy Saturday afternoon.

If you would like to set the next party, holiday, or special occasion off with a BANG! or if you just like to express yourself by making lots of noise, this is, without doubt, the project for you. Gather up all your tools and materials, send out advance warnings to parents, pets, aged relations and friends, and clear your working area so that it's ready for action.

Kids love them, parents hate them; whizz-bangers are the most amazing noisemakers that you ever did see. They are really good fun (FIG. 31-1).

MAKING TIME AND SKILL LEVEL

I would say that this project can easily be made by a nimble-fingered 8- to 12-year-old in about 30 minutes.

Cautions and adult help   No problems with this project, the tools are relatively safe to use and the making stages are easy-to-manage. If you have any worries about your child using a pair of scissors, be on hand and ready to help.

Be warned   Although our whizz-bangers are beautifully safe, they are very very noisy. Best let people of a nervous disposition know what's coming their way!

TOOLS AND MATERIALS

- [ ] A sheet of stiff cardboard about 12 inches long and 8 inches wide. You can use anything from a piece of cardboard salvaged from a breakfast cereal box to a piece of colored construction cardboard.
- [ ] A piece of strong paper 4 inches wide and 8 inches long. Best to use a color that contrasts with the cardboard
- [ ] A pencil and ruler   [ ] A pair of scissors   [ ] A glue pen
- [ ] A pack of lick-and-stick merit stars
- [ ] A roll of clear plastic sticky tape

MEASURE, MARK AND MAKE

I   Have a look at the project picture (FIG. 31-1) and the pattern page (FIG. 31-2), and see how the whizz-banger is made from cardboard and paper, with the card being the large diamond shape and the paper being the triangular pocket. Note how the small scraps of paper can be used as decorative trim.

Continued

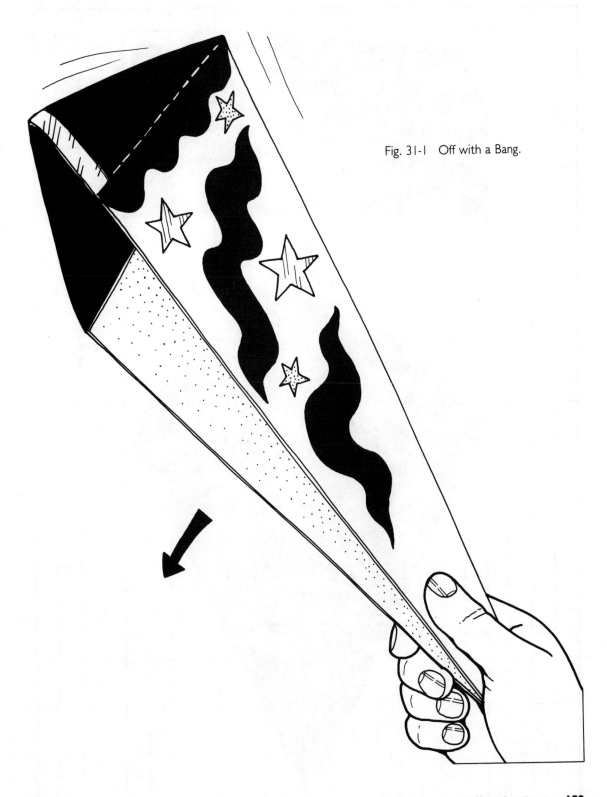

Fig. 31-1 Off with a Bang.

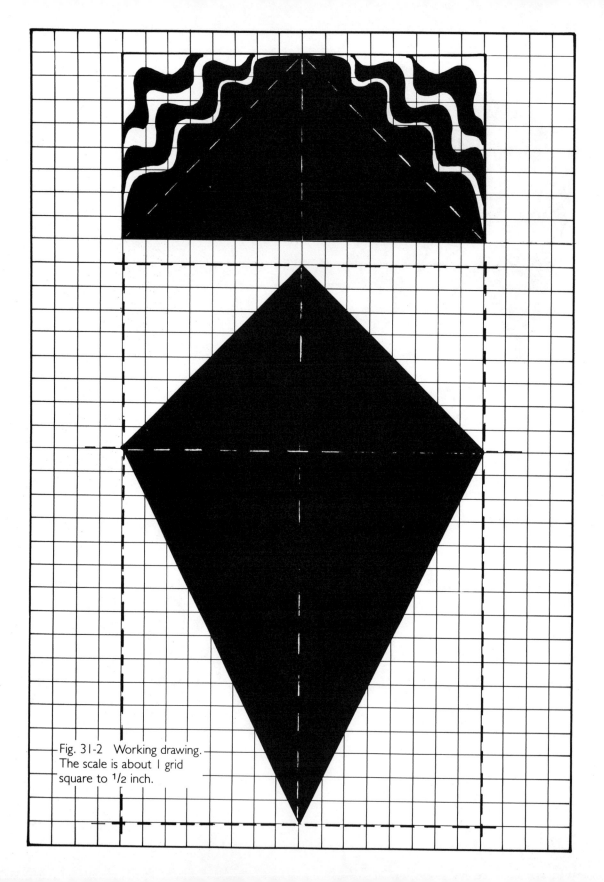

Fig. 31-2 Working drawing.
The scale is about 1 grid
square to 1/2 inch.

2 When you have a clear picture in your mind's eye of just how the project needs to be worked and put together, take the 12-×-8-inch piece of cardboard and carefully crease it in half down its length so that you have a book-fold that measures 12×4 inches (FIG. 31-3 top left).

3 Set the book-fold out on the worksurface so that the fold is to your left, then take a pencil and mark in a point 4 inches down the right-hand side; that is, down the long edge (FIG. 31-3 top left).

4 With the card still folded, use a pencil and ruler to set out the diamond shape. Draw in two straight lines, one from the top left-hand corner and down to the pencil point, and one from bottom left-hand corner and up. Cut off the corners of waste (FIG. 31-3 top middle left).

5 Take the 4-×-8-inch piece of paper, and fold it in half across its length so that you have a bookfold that measures 4×4 inches (FIG. 31-3 top middle right).

6 With the crease or fold to your left, take a pencil and ruler and draw in a diagonal line that runs from top left down to bottom right.

Continued

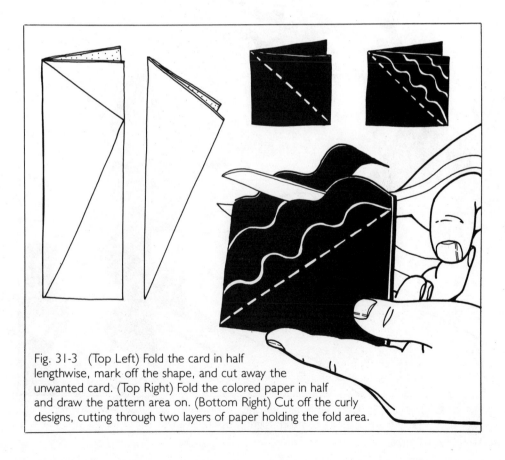

Fig. 31-3 (Top Left) Fold the card in half lengthwise, mark off the shape, and cut away the unwanted card. (Top Right) Fold the colored paper in half and draw the pattern area on. (Bottom Right) Cut off the curly designs, cutting through two layers of paper holding the fold area.

7   Allowing for a glue-fix fold-over that is at least $^1/_2$ inch wide, cut away the bulk of the waste and then use the scraps to make decorative trim pieces (FIG. 31-3 bottom right).

8   With the paper opened out and set best-face-down on the worksurface, take the card shape and arrange it best-face-up on the paper.

9   When you have made sure that the paper and card are well aligned, that is, with the long, straight edge of the paper running from point-to-point under the card shape, smear glue over the flaps and press them down (FIG. 31-4 top).

10   Making sure to stay well clear of the central fold, use the scraps and the merit stars to decorate the back of the banger.

11   Strengthen the long paper edge with a strip of clear sticky tape.

12   Finally, when you are ready for action, tuck in the paper pocket (FIG. 31-4 bottom), fold the card in half, then take the banger by the long tail and swish it hard through the air. The paper pocket will flip out and make a loud crack.

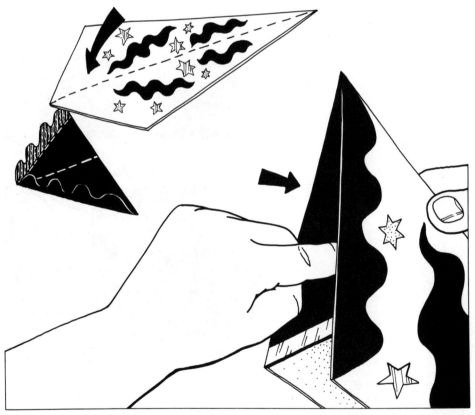

Fig. 31-4   (Top Left) Stick the paper banger onto the inside of the card, folding the top edges over and sticking them securely. (Bottom Right) Push the banger back into the fold and it is ready to use.

WATCH-POINTS AND FOLLOW-UPS

○ When you are choosing your materials, go for a medium-weight cardboard and a strong paper—brown wrapping paper works well.

○ Bearing in mind that the bigger the banger the bigger the bang, if you decide to change the size of the project, make sure that you stay within the overall paper-to-card proportions.

○ The cardboard needs to be stiff but flexible. Don't use corrugated packaging cardboard or heavyweight book-binding board.

32

Criss-Cross Christmas

A cross-stitch Christmas card

Cross-stitch is a beautifully simple embroidery technique—all you need is a needle, a supply of colored thread or floss, and a piece of cross-stitch fabric that is already marked off in squares. A single cross is made by selecting a group of four squares and by sewing in-and-out diagonals; it's that easy. By using different-colored threads and by grouping the crosses, it's possible to create characteristic stepped designs—a really good technique for working lettered samplers and small pictures.

If you are looking to make a small picture design for a greeting card, say, for a Christmas card, then cross-stitch is for you. Okay, enough of the praise-and-promise, now's the time to gather all your tools and materials and get down to work. If you want to know more about cross-stitch, I would say that grandma is the person to ask!

MAKING TIME AND SKILL LEVEL

Cross-stitch embroidery is easy—and I do mean *easy*. If you can push a blunt needle in-and-out a ready-made hole, and if you can count up to four, then I would say that there's going to be no stopping you. Of course, you do have to take it nice and easy, but that said, I'd say that the average 7- to-12-year-old kid could have this project all wrapped in about 30 minutes.

Cautions and adult help   If you are a beginner, you might need help starting and finishing. Ask an adult to start you off and to make checks at the end of every row of crosses.

Be warned   Craft knives need to be very sharp; best ask an adult to cut the card for you.

Even blunt needles can be dangerous. Watch out for your eyes, and make sure that you put the needle back when you have finished with it.

TOOLS AND MATERIALS

☐ A piece of open-weave cross-stitch fabric or Aida cloth at about 4×4 inches
☐ Embroidery thread/floss in three colors: red, green, and a color to match your chosen beads

Continued

Fig. 32-1 Criss-Cross Christmas.

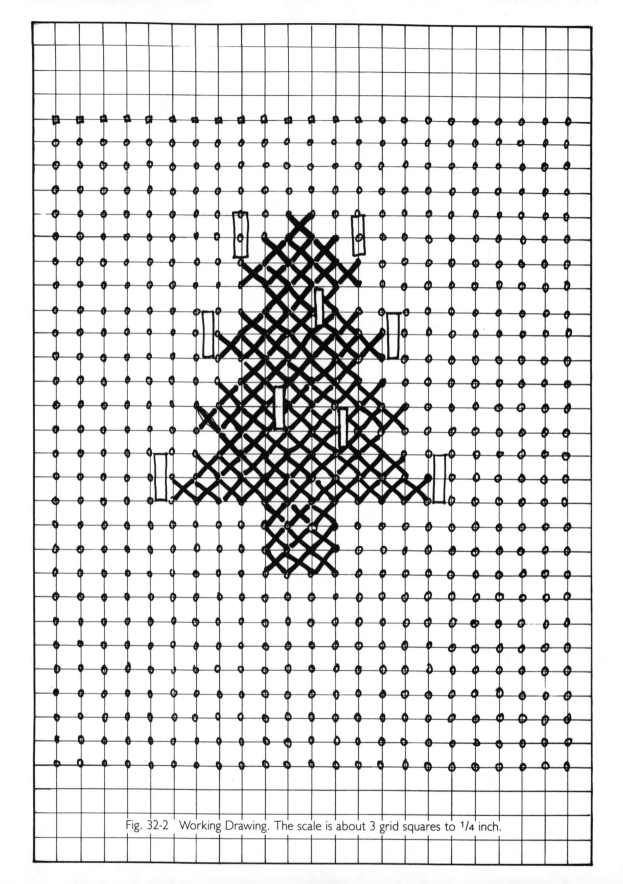

Fig. 32-2 Working Drawing. The scale is about 3 grid squares to ¼ inch.

☐ A big-eyed embroidery needle
☐ About 10 small beads; best if they are brightly colored and tube-shaped
☐ A sheet of thin card at about 6 1/2 × 10 inches
☐ A pencil and ruler ☐ A pair of scissors ☐ A sharp craft knife
☐ A metal cutting ruler ☐ A roll of double-sided sticky tape

MEASURE, MARK AND MAKE

1 Have a good look at the project picture (FIG. 32-1) and the working pattern (FIG. 32-2), and see how the holes in the special cross-stitch fabric are marked out in squares. Note how the Christmas tree design is made up from carefully counted and placed rows of crosses.

2 When you have a good understanding of how the crosses are worked, thread the needle up with green thread and mark your starting hole.

Continued

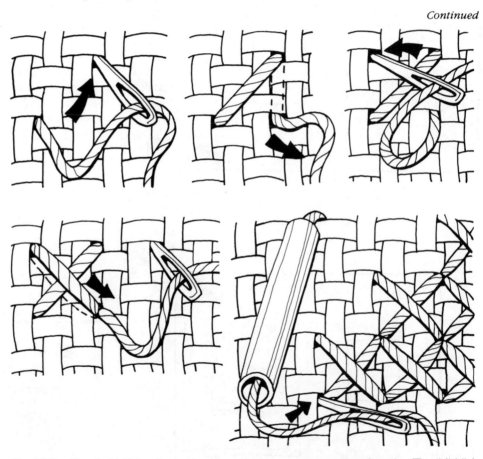

Fig. 32-3 (Top Left) Take the embroidery thread over two color threads. (Top Middle) Come down behind two. (Top Right) Cross over the first stitch over two cloth threads. (Bottom Left) Then back under to emerge at same spot. (Bottom Right) Position the thread carefully and pass the needle and thread through it, back through the cloth.

3 Starting at the back of the fabric, draw the thread through the bottom left-hand corner of the first square, and pass it down through the top right-hand corner (FIG. 32-3 top left).

4 With the needle now at the back of the fabric, draw the thread through the bottom right-hand corner of the square (FIG. 32-3 top middle).

5 Pass the needle down through the top right-hand corner of the square so as to complete the first cross-stitch (FIG. 32-3 top right).

6 And so you continue, criss-crossing the yarn in and out, until you have finished the design (FIG. 32-3 bottom left).

Continued

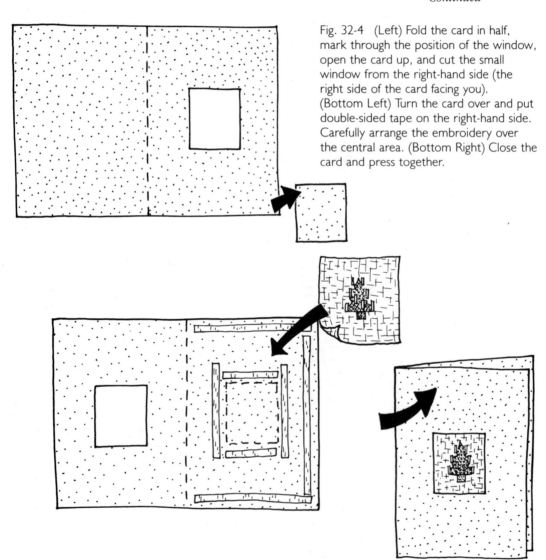

Fig. 32-4 (Left) Fold the card in half, mark through the position of the window, open the card up, and cut the small window from the right-hand side (the right side of the card facing you). (Bottom Left) Turn the card over and put double-sided tape on the right-hand side. Carefully arrange the embroidery over the central area. (Bottom Right) Close the card and press together.

7 When you have finished the design, take the needle threaded up with the bead-colored floss, and sew the beads on. Draw the needle up from the back of the fabric, through a bead, and back down through the fabric (FIG. 32-3 bottom right).

8 When you come to mounting the finished cross-stitch, crease the card in half so as to make a book-fold that measures about 6 1/2 × 5 inches, and then carefully cut out the embroidery window (FIG. 32-4 top left).

9 With the card opened and best-face-down on the worksurface, mark out the position of the fabric, then edge the card and the cut-out window with strips of double-sided sticky tape (FIG. 32-4 bottom left).

10 Set the cross-stitch down on the double-sided sticky tape, making sure that it is well placed. Then fold the card up so that the embroidery is sandwiched and looks to be nicely framed (FIG. 32-4 bottom right).

WATCH-POINTS AND FOLLOW-UPS

◯ If you are a beginner, you could mark out the crosses and the overall outline with a soft pencil.

◯ If you like the idea of cross-stitch, best get yourself a little embroidery frame— it's easier if the fabric is taut.

◯ When your adult helper comes to cutting out the card window, make sure that the window is larger than the cross-stitch design, but smaller than the piece of fabric—even adults make mess-ups!

33

Badge Button Banner

Badge banner

My kids like collecting badges and buttons. You know the sort of thing: "Big Is Beautiful," "Ban the Bomb," "Keep the Earth Green," and so on. Well after they had about 200 badges, we all knew that it was time to stop making holes in the bedroom walls and start pinning the badges on banners. After much discussion, it was decided that badges, broaches, buttons, and pin-stickers are best grouped according to type, size, or color, and then hung on a small felt shield-shaped display banner.

Badge collections look really good when they are sorted out and displayed as a nicely mounted unit. Maybe you could make a banner for your school or for your club—they look really good. You could have a red felt shield banner for car badges, a yellow shield for, say, army badges, and so on. Badge banners are a great idea!

MAKING TIME AND SKILL LEVEL

This is really a very basic and easy project to make. A 6- to 12-year-old could have a banner made in under 30 minutes.

Cautions and adult help   Although the decorative knots look complicated, they are, in fact, easy and straightforward. Best practice first and then ask for adult help if you need it.

Be warned   Needles are sharp. Keep them away from your eyes, and away from pets and smaller brothers and sisters.

TOOLS AND MATERIALS

☐ A piece of felt as large as you like
☐ A length of 1/2-inch-diameter dowel to fit the felt
☐ A ball of smooth cotton cord
☐ A large round-point needle with an eye big enough to take the cord
☐ A pair of scissors   ☐ A few tabs of sticky tape

Fig. 33-1   Badge Button Banner.

MEASURE, MARK AND MAKE

1   Have a look at the project picture (FIG. 33-1) and the working drawing (FIG. 33-2) and see how the banner is made and put together. Note the way the dowel has been threaded through the slots, and how the ends of the dowel have been decorated with simple "Turk's Head" knots.

2   When you have decided how big you want your banner to be, trace off the design and pencil-press-transfer the traced lines through to the felt.

Continued

Badge Button Banner   171

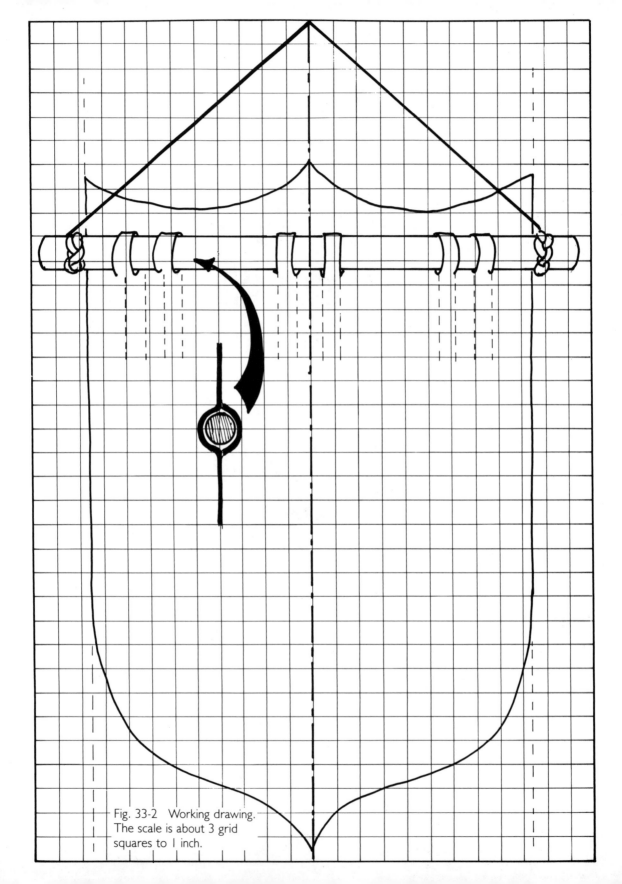

Fig. 33-2 Working drawing.
The scale is about 3 grid
squares to 1 inch.

3 Cut out the basic shield shape, then turn the top of the felt shape over and carefully mark and cut the twelve dowel slots. Keep the slots small so that the dowel is a tight fit (FIG. 33-3 top).

4 Thread the dowel in-and-out through the slots (FIG. 33-3 bottom).

5 When you come to tying the first Turk's head knot, thread up a good length of cotton cord, and start by fixing the end of the cord to the dowel with a tab of sticky tape (FIG. 33-4 top left).

6 Take the cord around the dowel so that it crosses over itself (FIG. 33-4 top, second from left).

7 Continue around—thread the needle under the top right-hand arm of the cross (FIG. 33-4 top, second from right).

8 Continue around the dowel—push the needle under the cross and ease the right-hand cord under the one on the left (FIG. 33-4 top right).

9 Once you have eased a loop of right-hand cord under the cross, pass the needle under-and-up through the loop (FIG. 33-4 bottom left).

10 Continue around the dowel—pass the needle under the top right arm of the cross (FIG. 33-4 bottom, second from left).

Continued

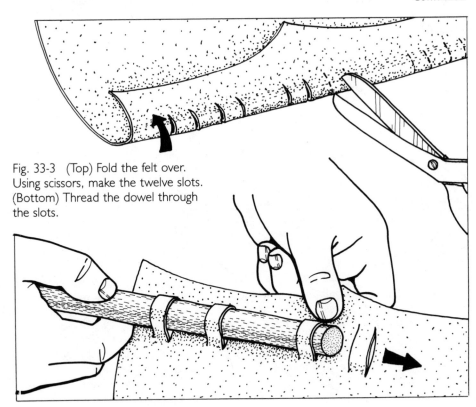

Fig. 33-3 (Top) Fold the felt over. Using scissors, make the twelve slots. (Bottom) Thread the dowel through the slots.

11 Pass the needle through under from the left side (FIG. 33-4 bottom, second from right).

12 Remove the small tab of sticky tape and work around the knot, carefully following the ''weave'' (FIG. 33-4 bottom right).

13 Finally, tie the ''hanging'' cord from one end of the dowel to the other, and the banner is ready for your badges.

WATCH-POINTS AND FOLLOW-UPS

○ If you want to make a much larger banner, you must use a thicker dowel.
○ If you want to make a long, thin banner, one big enough for all your badges, buy a roll of felt or use another nonfray fabric.

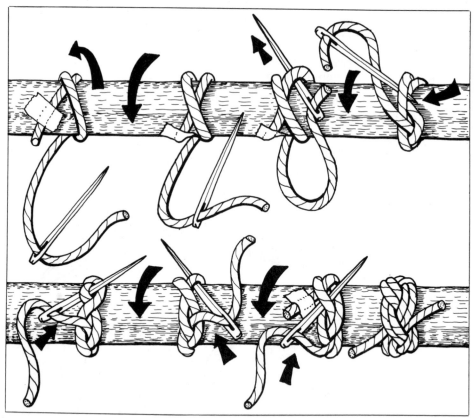

Fig. 33-4 (Top, left to right) Secure one end of cord with tape to the dowel and wind the cord around so that it crosses over itself. Turn the dowel over towards you. Take the cord under the top right-hand arm of the cross. Turn the dowel over towards you; with the bodkin, ease the top right-hand cord under the one on the left. (Bottom, left to right) Pass the cord under the ''moved'' loop. Turn the dowel over towards you and pass the cord under the top right ''arm'' of the cross. Turn the dowel again and pass the cord through and under from the left side. Take off the tape and continue following the ''weave,'' being careful not to cross over the cord you are following. (Bottom Right) The finished knot.

34

Eggciting Fashion
Egghead fashion model dolls

Our egghead fashion models are the snappiest dressers you ever did see. With their full, gathered skirts and huge, wide-brimmed, flower-decorated hats, they really are beautiful. Our dolls are so "eggclusive," our dolls are "eggceptional." They really are hard-boiled "egghibitionists."

Egghead dolls are a really good-fun idea. All you do is take a hard-boiled egg and a few scraps of cardboard and fabric, and then set about making a little egghead character. The good-fun bit is giving the doll a name, title, or description that contains the word "egg." So, for example, you might give your egg a crown and title her "Your Eggcellency," or you could give your little egg a hat, a back pack, and big boots and give him the title "Eggsplorer."

Have fun . . . egg heads are so "eggciting," so "eggceptional," and so "eggpressive!"

MAKING TIME AND SKILL LEVEL

Although Egghead dolls are very easy to make, giving them names and titles can be a bit tricky, this part of the project is really aimed at older children. But then again, you can leave out the names and the titles bit, and you can make the doll designs as simple or as complicated as you wish. A 6- to 12-year-old will be able to make one of our little dolls in about 10 to 20 minutes.

Cautions and adult help The dresses and hats are easy, but do you know how to cook a hard-boiled egg? If you have never cooked a hard-boiled egg before, then best ask an adult or an older brother or sister to show you how.

Be warned Boiling water is dangerous—do not try to cook the egg without adult help.

TOOLS AND MATERIALS

☐ A hard-boiled egg in an eggcup
☐ A few scraps of pretty, lightweight cotton fabric
☐ A piece of thin cardboard   ☐ A needle and cotton   ☐ A pair of scissors
☐ A pencil, ruler, and compass   ☐ A tube of clear quick-set glue
☐ A few scraps of pink and green crepe paper
☐ A pack of colored felt-tip pens
☐ Feathers for trim

Fig. 34-1. Eggciting Fashions.

MEASURE, MARK AND MAKE

1 Have a look at the project picture (FIG. 34-1) and the working drawing (FIG. 34-2) and see how easily the eggs are dressed and decorated.

2 Work out the skirt measurements by placing the hard-boiled egg in the eggcup and measuring—from the top of the eggcup down to the table, and 2½ times around the egg (FIG. 34-3 top left).

Continued

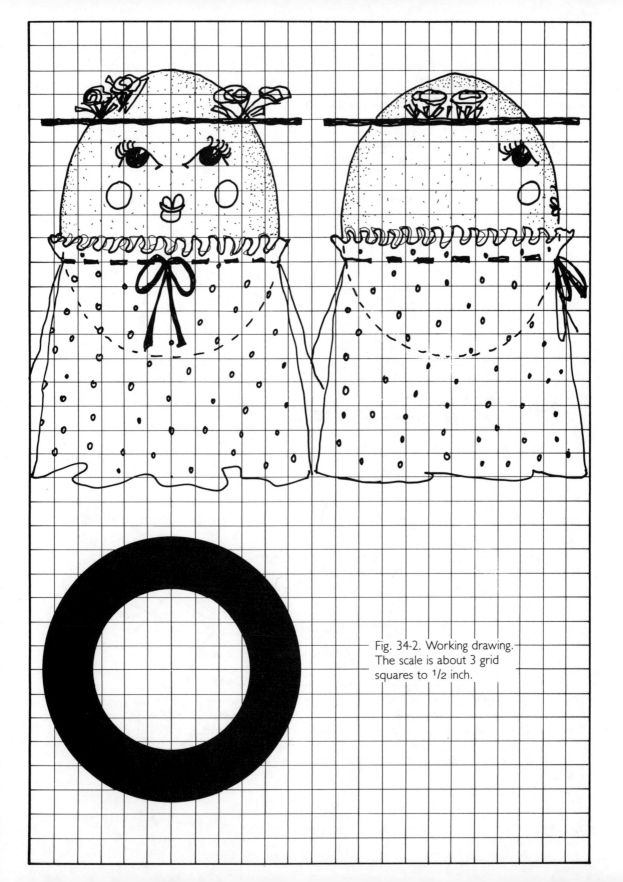

Fig. 34-2. Working drawing.
The scale is about 3 grid
squares to 1/2 inch.

3 Cut out the skirt material.

4 Use the pencil, ruler, and compass to draw the hat brim out on the card. Be very careful when you come to cutting out the inner hat circle; best cut out a little at a time, until the hat is a good fit (FIG. 34-3 top right).

5 Thread the needle, and sew in-and-out along one long edge of the skirt fabric. Leave the cotton ends long so that they can be tied around the egg (FIG. 34-3 bottom right).

6 When you come to making the flowers, cut and roll a little strip of pink crepe paper; pinch and glue the bottom and spread the top to make the petals (FIG. 34-4 top).

Continued

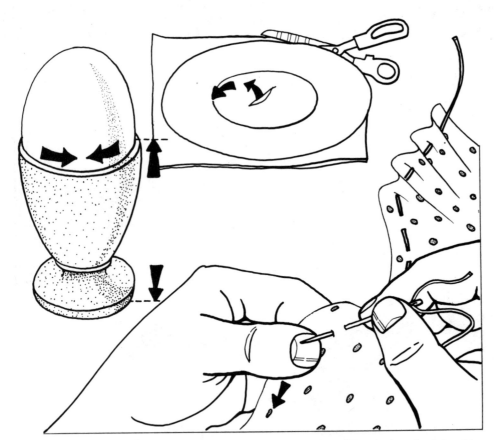

Fig. 34-3. (Left) Place the cooked egg in the eggcup, and measure for the length of the skirt from top of eggcup to tabletop, and for the width approximately 2 1/2 times around the egg. (Top Right) Draw a circle for the hat rim and cut the inner circle away carefully, a little at a time, fitting it on the egg to get the correct size. (Bottom Right) Gather the skirt material, using a needle and thread. Be sure to leave the thread with long ends so that they can be tied around the egg.

7 To make the leaves: cut a strip of green crepe paper and sew in-and-out along one edge, and gather to make tight bunches (FIG. 34-4 top).

8 Finally, glue the flowers and leaves on the hat and use the felt-tip pens to color in the feathers.

Fig. 34-4. (Top) Roll the pink crepe paper to make the flowers by pinching the bottom and spreading the top to make the petals. Cut the regular slots along the length of the green for the leaves and gather with a needle and thread to form bunches of leaves. (Bottom) Glue the leaves, flowers, and bow on. Using a felt-tip pen, draw in the features of the fashion model.

WATCH-POINTS AND FOLLOW-UPS

○ Egghead dolls are a good idea for parties and picnics; you can dress and name the dolls/eggs, and use them instead of place setting cards.

○ Make sure that the eggs are clean, cool, and dry before you start dressing them.

○ If the eggshells are a bit waxy, they won't take the felt-tip colors; give them a wipe-over with a spot of washing-up liquid.

35

Basil Balloon
Balloon-head party-time dolls

Good old Basil Balloon, he's the life and soul of the party. He doesn't say much, and maybe he doesn't join in, but then again, Basil reckons that just having him around is enough to set the party swinging. Basil is a great mover, he just loves to stand and gently sway in time to the music. With his big, beautiful eyes, large smiling mouth and ever-tapping feet, Basil never gets anxious or over-excited—he's a real cool cat. Of course, it has been said that Basil is a bit of an empty head—you know, all show and not much between his ears—but don't you believe it, he's a great guy to have around. Next time you are having a party, why don't you make a few balloon heads. They are great fun!

It's worth saying at this point, that Basil hates needles, pins, and the like. Would you believe that the very sight of a pin is enough to make him really unhappy and completely deflated?

MAKING TIME AND SKILL LEVEL

Balloon heads are very easy to make; a balloon and few scraps of card and paper, and the project is more than half made. Most 6- to 12-year-olds will have Basil made and smiling in about 20 to 30 minutes.

Cautions and adult help You won't need help with this project; it's easy and it's safe.

Be warned Once the paper cutouts have been stuck down, they are best left alone; if you try to remove the double-sided sticky tape, the balloons will burst.

TOOLS AND MATERIALS
- ☐ A large round balloon for each character that you want to make
- ☐ A good supply of thick and thin colored cardboard scraps
- ☐ A roll of double-sided sticky tape ☐ A sheet of tracing paper
- ☐ A pencil and ruler ☐ A paper punch

MEASURE, MARK AND MAKE

1 First have a good look at the project picture (FIG. 35-1) and the working drawing (FIG. 35-2), and see how the balloon heads are made and put together. See how the various cutouts are fixed with double-sided sticky tape. See also how the balloon is held and supported by the large thick cardboard "feet."

Continued

Fig. 35-1   Basil Balloon.

Fig. 35-2 Working drawing. The scale is about I grid square to ¹/4 inch.

2 When you have looked at our design and maybe thought up a few ideas of your own, trace off all the shapes and pencil-press-transfer them through to your chosen pieces of colored paper and cardboard.

3 Take the "feet," trim up the shape of the toes and then use the punch to make the balloon hole.

4 Blow up the balloon, tie and knot the mouthpiece, and carefully pull the mouthpiece down through the punched hole and up through the between-feet slot (FIG. 35-3). ·

5 Take the "nose" cutout, roll it around to make a cone, and fix it with a tab of double-sided sticky tape (FIG. 35-4 top left).

6 With the two fixing tabs now on each side of the cone, bend the tabs over so that they are inside the cone and then fix them to the balloon with small pieces of sticky tape.

Continued

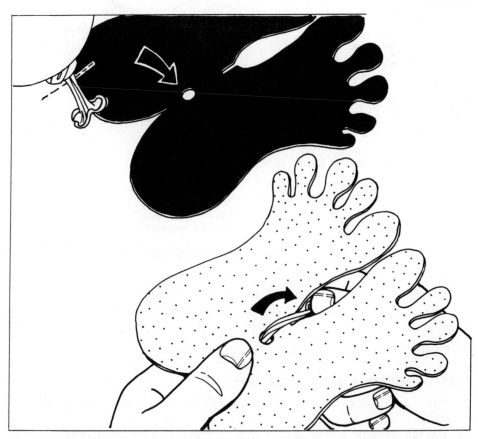

Fig. 35-3   (Top Left) Push the nozzle of the balloon through the hole in the foot from the top side. (Bottom Right) Turn "Basil" upside down and hold him by his feet, then stretch and push the nozzle along and back through the slot between the feet.

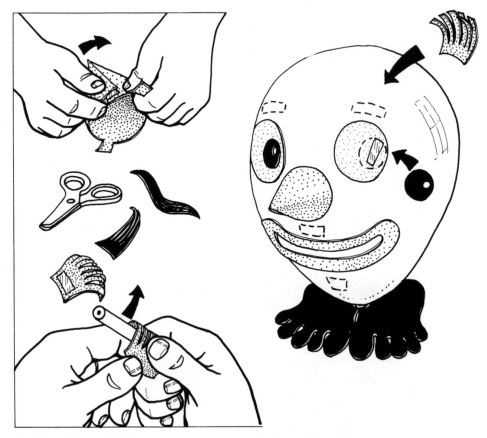

Fig. 35-4 (Top Left) Fold the nose into a cone shape by overlapping the straight sides, then tape with double-sided tape. (Middle Right) Using double-sided tape arrange the nose, eyes, and mouth on the balloon, making sure the toes face the front. (Bottom Left) To curl the eyebrows, moustache, and beard, stroke the paper between thumb and pencil.

7 Use tabs of double-sided sticky tape to fix the large "eye" disks and the "mouth" (FIG. 35-4 right).

8 Punch holes through the two small "eye pupils" and stick them in place on the large disk. Have the punched holes both looking in the same direction (FIG. 35-4 right).

9 Finally, cut, fit, and fix the other features (FIG. 35-4).

WATCH-POINTS AND FOLLOW-UPS

○ If you decide to use a much larger balloon, make sure that you make the feet larger.

○ You can continue adding cutouts until your character has eyes, a nose, a moustache, glasses, ears, hair, a hat, and so on.

○ Think very carefully how you want the cutouts placed. Once they are stuck down, they are almost impossible to move.

Plait Mats
A braided and sewn table- or placemat

Rag braiding or plaiting is easy; it's child's play! Three lengths of clean cotton rag are folded, braided, twisted into whorls, and finally stitched into rounds. The resulting flat whorl makes a really good kitchen hearth-type table mat. With a few plait mats scattered about, hot pots and pans won't harm the table. Also, after the meal is over, the mats can simply be shaken to remove any bits of food.

If you get to like the idea of folding, plaiting, and sewing, then you can make your mat bigger and BIGGER! Or then again, if you can persuade all your friends, family, and neighbors to make little mats, then you could sew them together to make one huge rug. Plait mats are a good-fun idea!

MAKING TIME AND SKILL LEVEL

If you can plait and sew, then this is a very straightforward project. Plait mats are easy to make and you can use very ordinary around-the-house tools and materials. An average 7- to 12-year-old can make a small plate-size plait mat in about 2 hours. Best to do the plaiting one day, and the putting together the next.

Cautions and adult help Most children know how to do 3-strand braiding or plaiting—it's the sort of skill they pick at school. If you don't know how to braid, ask a friend to show you how. After about 10 minutes you will soon get the hang of it.

If you are a beginner, practice with three different color strands. Be sure to keep the tension even.

Be warned Sewing the mat is a little bit tricky. Aim for small hidden stitches, and watch out for that needle when you are trying to push it through the layered braids.

TOOLS AND MATERIALS

☐ A good supply of thin, clean, cotton rags; best to use strips torn from such items as old white sheets, and gingham skirts, shirts, and curtains. You need three strips of fabric, one light and two dark.

☐ A pair of scissors ☐ A length of cord ☐ A needle and thread

MEASURE, MARK AND MAKE

1   Start by having a good look at the project picture (FIG. 36-1) and the working pattern (FIG. 36-2). See how the strips of fabric are folded and plaited/braided. Also note how the plait is coiled and sewn.

2   Select your fabric and tear off three strips, each 2 inches wide and 58 inches long. You need two dark strips and one light (FIG. 36-3 top).

3   Fold and roll each strip of fabric side-to-middle so that the frayed edges are hidden (FIG. 36-3 middle).

4   Gather the strips together at one end, and tie them, say, to a hook in the wall or a large piece of furniture (FIG. 36-3 bottom).

5   Pull the three strips towards you so that they are tight, then fold one or other of the outside strips over the central strip (FIG. 36-4 top left).

Continued

Fig. 36-1   Plait Mat.

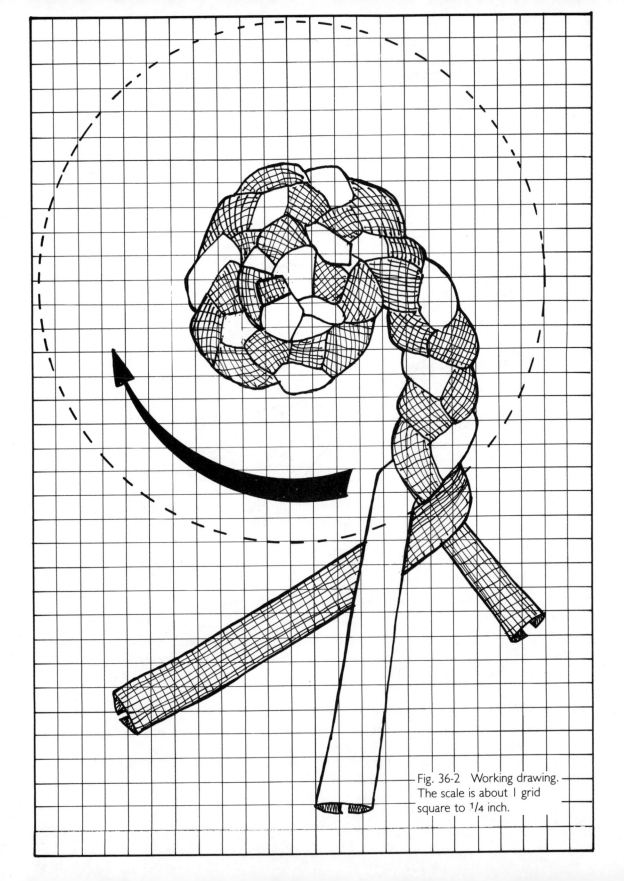

Fig. 36-2 Working drawing. The scale is about 1 grid square to 1/4 inch.

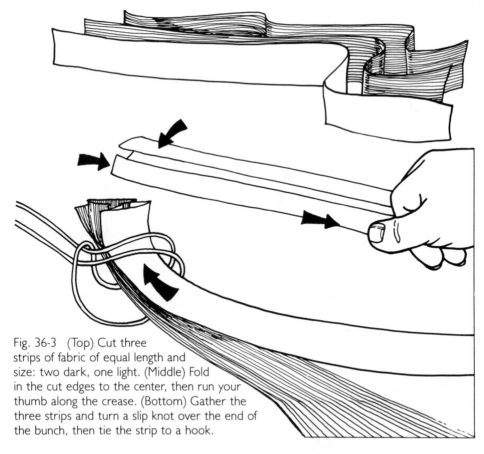

Fig. 36-3 (Top) Cut three strips of fabric of equal length and size: two dark, one light. (Middle) Fold in the cut edges to the center, then run your thumb along the crease. (Bottom) Gather the three strips and turn a slip knot over the end of the bunch, then tie the strip to a hook.

6 Continue plaiting the three strips—left over middle, right over middle, left over middle, and so on—with all three strips changing places to become in turn "left," "right," and "middle" (FIG. 36-4 top right).

7 Tidy up the shape of the plait as you go along. Don't let go of the bit that you have plaited (FIG. 36-4 bottom).

8 When you have finished the plait, sew off the ends to stop them from coming undone.

9 Roll the plait up into a flat coil or spiral shape, and carefully sew the braid to itself when you have finished the round, tuck in all the loose ends and do several over-and-over stitches to finish off (FIG. 36-5).

WATCH-POINTS AND FOLLOW-UPS

○ If, when you are plaiting, you want to have several rests along the way, secure the bit that you have done with a large gripper-type paper clip.
○ When you come to sewing up the coil, use a matching color thread. Try to keep the stitches small and hidden.

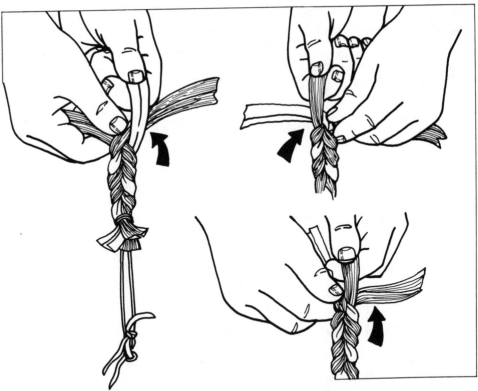

Fig. 36-4 (Top Left) Pull the plait towards you so that the strips are tight. Fold the outside strip over the center strip. (Top Right) Continue plaiting—left over middle—right over middle, and so on. (Bottom) Hold the plait firmly and tidy up the shape as you go along.

Fig. 36-5 Sew the plait in a spiral shape, starting from the center. When you come to the end on the outside, over-sew any rough edges.

37

Penny Peeps
A traditional peep-show box

The Victorians loved peep shows, which involved a large mysterious box, a handle, a slot for pennies, and a little viewing window. The penny was dropped in the slot, the handle was turned, and presto! the picture images flickered, moved, and appeared to come to life. Of course, it was all really very simple—just hundreds of drawings being spun around—but the wonderful thing is that these very same fun and fantasy pleasure machines led to the invention of films and television.

Our little peep show is good fun. You hold it up to the window and look through the peep-hole, and there you see a little stage set—a sky, clouds, bushes, and a couple of rabbits, all bathed in a cool green-glade light and looking very realistic.

Peep shows are exciting. If you are interested and want more information, ask your teachers, or better still, make contact with the oldest person you can find and ask them!

MAKING TIME AND SKILL LEVEL

A peep show is not a difficult project, but it does need to be made slowly and carefully. I would say that a 6- to 12-year-old could have the project made in a morning.

Cautions and adult help Although all the various making stages are easy enough, you will need some adult help when you come to putting the project together.

Be warned No problems with this project, just make sure that you keep the glue and scissors away from your younger brothers and sisters, and away from pets.

TOOLS AND MATERIALS
- [ ] An empty shoebox
- [ ] A small amount of thin cardboard, in cream and two shades of green
- [ ] A pencil and ruler [ ] A pair of scissors
- [ ] Acrylic paint in two shades of green [ ] A stack of old magazines
- [ ] A small amount of dark green tissue paper [ ] A few gathered twigs
- [ ] A pack of colored felt-tip pens
- [ ] A tube of quick-set general-purpose glue

Fig. 37-1   Penny Peeps.

Fig. 37-2 Working drawing. The scale is about I grid square to ¹/4 inch.

MEASURE, MARK AND MAKE

1 Have a look at the project picture (FIG. 37-1) and the working drawing (FIG. 37-2) and see how the little stage set is built into the box. Note the way the various bush, tree, and rabbit cutouts are mounted and displayed.

2 Paint the inside of the shoebox dark green, then use a little light-green paint to flick and texture the dark green so as to make a green grass-type effect (FIG. 37-3 top left).

3 Look through old magazines and search out a forest glade scene. Glue the scene on the inside back end of the box (FIG. 37-3 top right).

4 Trace off the rabbits and bushes, and then pencil-press-transfer the traced lines through to the working face of the card. Have the bushes green and rabbits cream-colored (FIG. 37-3 bottom).

Continued

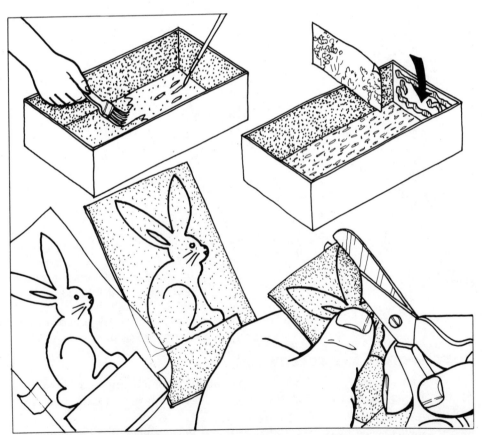

Fig. 37-3   (Top Left) Paint the inside of the box green and texture it with a light green, using a fine brush. (Top Right) Glue a forest scene cut out from a magazine to the back of the box. (Bottom) Trace and pencil-press-transfer the lines of the designs onto colored card. Cut out the profiles.

5 Make a small slot in the front of the box for a peephole, and have a scattering of holes in the lid; make the small holes by pushing the point of a pencil through the cardboard into a ball of Plasticine. (FIG. 37-4 top).

6 Have a look at the plan to see how the various bits and pieces are arranged. Bend the "glue" tabs of the bush cutouts over and stick them to the base and sides. Crinkle the green tissue into a ball and stick it down to make a green-grass rabbit warren effect. Stick the rabbit cutouts down, along with small bits of twig to make logs and branches (FIG. 37-4 bottom).

7 Finally, fit the lid on top of the box and the project is made.

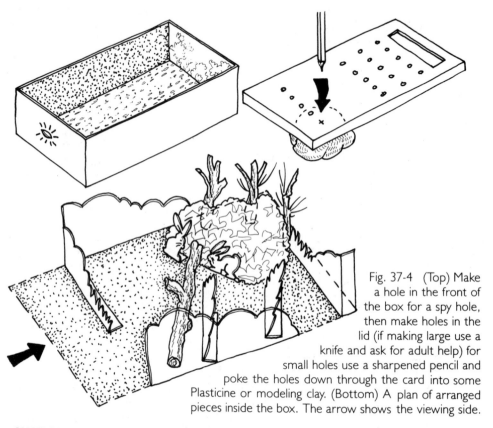

Fig. 37-4 (Top) Make a hole in the front of the box for a spy hole, then make holes in the lid (if making large use a knife and ask for adult help) for small holes use a sharpened pencil and poke the holes down through the card into some Plasticine or modeling clay. (Bottom) A plan of arranged pieces inside the box. The arrow shows the viewing side.

WATCH-POINTS AND FOLLOW-UPS

○ If you can't find a good shoebox, you could use a much larger cut-down box.
○ If you like the idea of peep shows, but don't much like rabbits, you could make just about any scene that you fancy.
○ You could take a huge box into school and make a gigantic classroom peep show—and make all your friends pay (with play money) for a peep.
○ When you are making the top-of-box light holes, best make few holes and then have a look, make a few more holes and have another look, and so on until you get the lighting just right.

Clowning Around
A clown-up-a-rope working toy

Clarence the climbing clown is as funny as funny can be! Hold the top end of the string in one hand and repeatedly pull down on the other, and Clarence will slowly heave himself up the rope. Amazing! Wonderful! Your friends will be sure to ask how the toy works. Well, just tell them that it's all done with strings, pulleys, and levers. Show your teacher the finished toy and see if he or she can tell you how and why Clarence is such a clever climber.

Anyway, you don't need to worry too much about the how's and why's, all you really need to know is that the climbing clown is an amazingly clever and agile athlete. If you can keep pulling the right strings, he can climb all day.

If you are looking to make a really good traditional Victorian working toy, this is the project for you.

MAKING TIME AND SKILL LEVEL

Although the various steps and stages are relatively simple, I would say that, overall, this project is best worked by older kids, or by a kids-and-adults team. From start to finish, Clarence can easily be made and put together by older children in the space of a morning.

Cautions and adult help   Although there are no problems as far as safety is concerned, you might need help when you come to putting Clarence together. Best go it alone for all the measuring, marking, and painting, and then get adult help for the cutting out and the final putting-together stages.

TOOLS AND MATERIALS

- ☐ A sheet of thick cardboard at about 12×12 inches. Use a stiff 1/8-inch-thick cardboard.
- ☐ A pencil and ruler   ☐ A sheet of tracing paper
- ☐ An elastic band; best have half a dozen in all different sizes.
- ☐ A pair of scissors   ☐ A packet of brass bend-tab paper fasteners
- ☐ A paper punch   ☐ A plastic drinking straw
- ☐ A selection of acrylic paints   ☐ A tube of quick-set adhesive
- ☐ A 24-inch length of 1/8-inch-diameter cord

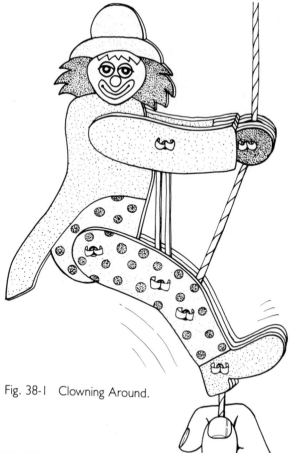

Fig. 38-1 Clowning Around.

MEASURE, MARK AND MAKE

1 Have a look at the project picture (FIG. 38-1) and the working drawing details (FIGS. 38-2 and FIG. 38-3), and see how the clown is made and put together. Note the fixed arms, the pivotal legs, the way the elastic band links the arms and the legs, and the route taken by the cord as it passes from the arms and through the legs.

2 Trace off the seven shapes that go to make up the design—the body, the two legs, the two arms, and the two hand-spacer pieces—and pencil-press-transfer the traced lines through to the 1/8-inch-thick cardboard.

3 Mark in the position of the various pivotal and fixing holes, and chop them out with the hole-punch. There should be two holes in each arm, four holes in each leg, one hole in the body, and one hole in each of the two hand-spacer pieces.

4 Clear the painting area and hang the seven cutouts up with pins and thread.

Continued

Fig. 38-2   Cutting Grid. The scale is about 1 grid square to ¼ inch.

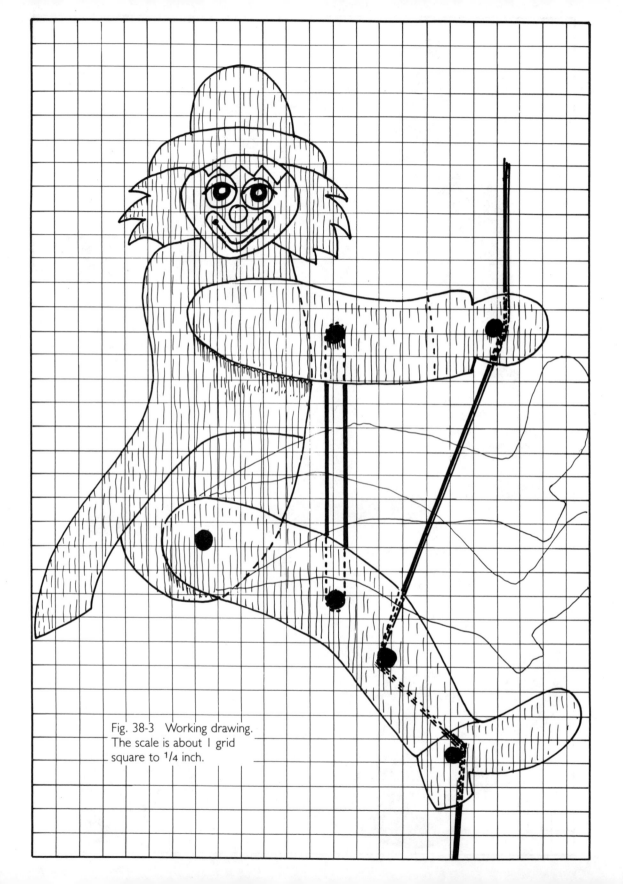

Fig. 38-3 Working drawing. The scale is about 1 grid square to ¼ inch.

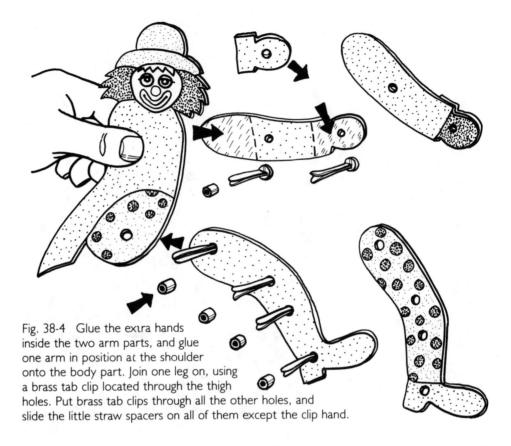

Fig. 38-4 Glue the extra hands inside the two arm parts, and glue one arm in position at the shoulder onto the body part. Join one leg on, using a brass tab clip located through the thigh holes. Put brass tab clips through all the other holes, and slide the little straw spacers on all of them except the clip hand.

5 When you come to painting, start by blocking in the large areas of background color—the trousers, jacket, hat and hair—and finish by dotting in the patterns and lining in the details.

6 When the paint is completely dry, set the body flat-down on the worksurface and start putting the bits together. Stick one arm in position on the body, pivot one leg, fit one hand spacer, and set the six brass tab clips in their holes (FIG. 38-4).

7 Cut three little lengths of plastic drinking straw to slide over the three leg clips, and set the elastic band in position from the arm to the leg (FIG. 38-5 top left).

8 Run the 1/8-inch-diameter cord from the arm, down-and-under the leg clip, and up-and-around the foot clip (FIG. 38-5 right).

Continued

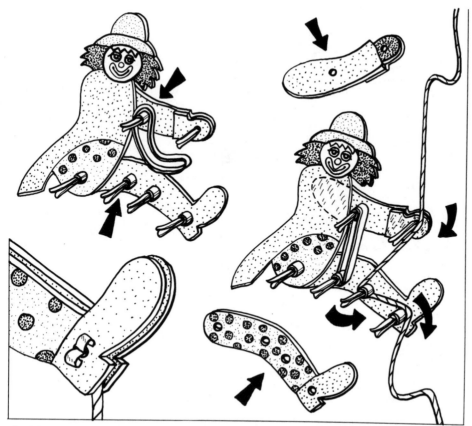

Fig. 38-5 (Top Left) Loop the rubber band over the top arm clip and the top of the leg clip below. (Right) Wind the string around the remaining arm and two leg clips. Slide the other arm in position, over the clips and bend them over. (Bottom Left) How the clips should look.

9 When you have stuck and fitted the other arm and hand spacer, and the other leg, bend and clench the brass clips (FIG. 38-5 bottom left).

10 Finally, when you come to testing out the clown—that is, when you come to pulling the ends of the cord apart—adjust as necessary the friction-fit of the cord through the hand spacers by tightening or loosening the hand clip.

WATCH-POINTS AND FOLLOW-UPS

○ If you like the idea of making a moving toy, but you are looking for something a bit stronger, you could use 1/8-inch-thick plywood and adjust the making stages accordingly.

○ If the arm and leg cutouts feel a bit floppy, use thicker cardboard or double up the card so that the arms and legs are two layers thick.

○ Don't worry if the cord-pulling working action is a bit stiff, it will loosen up with use.

Crazy Cog Creeper
An elastic-powered moon buggy

Quietly creeping and crawling over rough terrain, with cogged wheels clawing, whirring, and turning, our rubber band-powered moon buggy is an exciting working toy. Watch it climb out of the sandpit; watch it as it slowly drags its weary way across the dips and dunes of the bedcovers. Our moon vehicle is easy to make and fun to watch.

If you want to set off a craze at school, or get your science teacher excited, or use up all those odds and ends that you have cluttering up your cupboards, drawers, and cubbyholes, then this is the project for you.

Turn the pencil a dozen or so times in a counterclockwise direction, make sure that the wax friction-free bearing moves easily, set the cogged wheels down on the carpet, and the energy stored up in the rubber band is enough to drive the machine forward. Could it be bigger? Could it be smaller? Can it go faster? What fun!

MAKING TIME AND SKILL LEVEL

This is a project for older children. If all goes well—meaning if the wax doesn't break, if the elastic band is the correct length, and if the paint is acrylic and quick-drying—I would guess that a 10- to 12-year-old could put the moon buggy together in a couple of hours.

Cautions and adult help   Of all the projects in the book, this is probably one of the most tricky. This is not to say that the individual making stages are in any way difficult or dangerous, it's just that the project will only work if everything goes just right. You will need help when you come to putting the project together.

Be warned   Cutting the candle can be both difficult and dangerous. Best use a small-tooth junior-type hacksaw and to work on a chopping board.
Do not use a knife!

TOOLS AND MATERIALS
- [ ] A sheet of stiff cardboard at $3^1/2 \times 3^1/2$ inches
- [ ] A thread spool; it can be made of plastic or wood
- [ ] A fat rubber band   [ ] A domestic candle
- [ ] A matchstick and a pencil stub
- [ ] A small amount of double-sided sticky tape

Continued

□ A compass/pair of compasses   □ A pencil and ruler   □ A pair of scissors
□ A small junior-type hacksaw   □ A brush and acrylic paint
□ A hammer and a hole punch

MEASURE, MARK AND MAKE

I   Have a look at the project picture (FIG. 39-1) and the working drawing details (FIG. 39-2), and see how, from end to end, the parts are threaded on the rubber band placed in a particular order: matchstick, cog, spool, cog, wax washer, and pencil stub. Note how the cogs are stuck to the reel with tabs of double-sided tape.

2   Use the pencil and ruler to draw crossed diagonals on the 3½-inch-square pieces of cardboard.

Continued

Fig. 39-1   Crazy Cog Creeper.

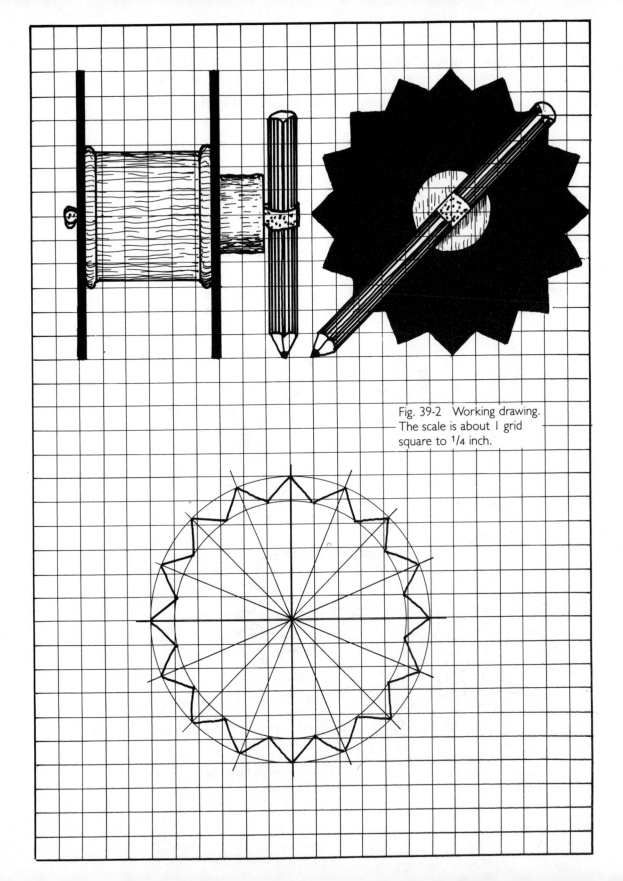

Fig. 39-2   Working drawing.
The scale is about 1 grid
square to 1/4 inch.

3 Set the compass first at a radius of 1½ inches and then at a radius of 1¼ inches, and draw the two circles that make up each cog (FIG. 39-3 top left).

4 Halve the quarter circles, then halve and halve again, until both circles are divided up into 16 slices or step-offs (FIG. 39-3 top).

5 Halve each of the step-offs—that is, each of the step-offs on the inner circle—and use a ruler to draw in the zigzag cog teeth (FIG. 39-3 top right).

6 When you have cut away the little triangles of waste, use the hammer punch to cut a hole at the center of each cog (FIG. 39-3 bottom left).

7 Being very careful not to crack or bend the candle, take the small hacksaw and cut a ½-inch-thick slice from the bottom of the candle. Cut around and around, and gently ease the wick out until you have a sort of fat wax washer (FIG. 39-3 bottom right).

8 When you have made the wax washer and both cogs, put a couple of tabs of double-sided sticky tape on each end of the spool and press the two cogs into position.

Continued

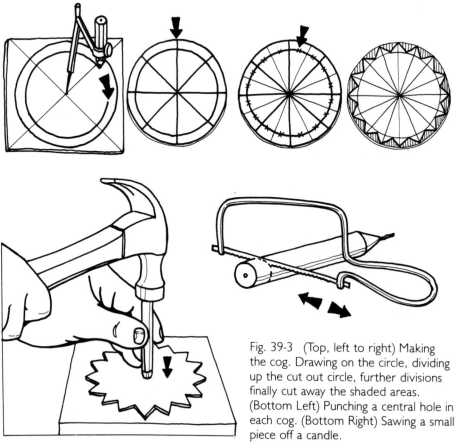

Fig. 39-3 (Top, left to right) Making the cog. Drawing on the circle, dividing up the cut out circle, further divisions finally cut away the shaded areas. (Bottom Left) Punching a central hole in each cog. (Bottom Right) Sawing a small piece off a candle.

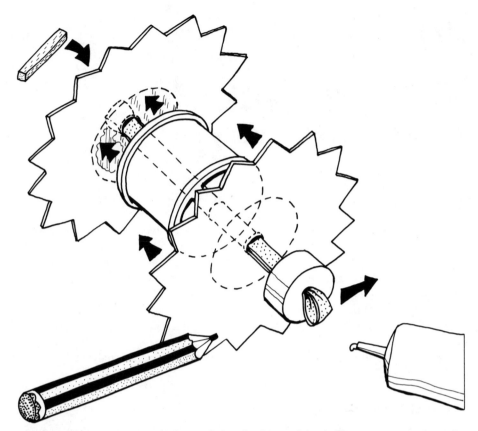

Fig. 39-4 Assembling the cog before painting (having a trial go). The cogs are stuck to the spool, the rubber band is threaded through the central hole, and on one side a piece of matchstick is threaded through the rubber band and glued against the cog. The other end of the band is passed through the candle and pencil is put through the end loop.

9 Thread the rubber band through the cogged spool and fit-and-fix the wax washer and the pencil stub. The threading order on the elastic band from the pencil stub end is: pencil, wax washer, cog, tabs of sticky tape, spool, tabs of sticky tape, cog, and matchstick (FIG. 39-4).

10 Finally, when you have made sure that the machine works, paint and decorate the spool and the cogs.

WATCH-POINTS AND FOLLOW-UPS

○ If you don't much like the idea of using a pencil, compass, and ruler to make the cogs, you could use a couple of plastic lids and cut the cog teeth by eye.

○ If the rubber band is so strong that the matchstick slides around, fix the matchstick to the cog with a dab of glue.

○ When you are painting, be careful not to get paint on the rubber band.

40
Wibble Wobble
A wibble-wobble Kelly doll

Kids love tumble dolls! Known in England as "Wibble-Wobbles" and in America as "Kellys" or "Tumblers," wibble-wobble tumble dolls are really great fun. Our doll is a likable easy-come, easy-go sort of character. Give her a knock and up she pops again. Tap her off her feet, and immediately she does a lazy-crazy sort of dance and then wobbles upright. But don't think for one moment that our tumble doll is a pushover; in fact, she is a totally dependable, completely steadfast lady who always springs back up again. She is well able to stand on her own two feet.

If you are looking to make a really good toy, say, a little plaything for yourself or an office toy for your mom or dad, then I've got a feeling that this is the project for you.

Our tumble doll lady is an easy-to-make good-fun traditional toy. She's beautiful!

MAKING TIME AND SKILL LEVEL

This is a very simple and straightforward project. I would say that most 6- to 12-year-olds will have their dolls made and tumbling in about 30 to 50 minutes.

Cautions and adult help   Ping-Pong balls are delicate; best plan out the project yourself, and then ask an adult to help you with the final putting-together stages.

Be warned   Glues and adhesives are both sticky and tricky; be very careful. Make sure that your glue is okay to use with ping pong type plastics.

TOOLS AND MATERIALS
- [ ] A couple of ordinary white table tennis or Ping-Pong balls
- [ ] A small amount of plaster of paris or decorator's filler
- [ ] A small handful of lead shot
- [ ] A piece of thin dowel at about 3 inches long; you could use an old pencil stub
- [ ] A tube of clear quick-set glue   [ ] A good selection of acrylic colors
- [ ] A couple of paint brushes—one broad and the other fine-point
- [ ] A small amount of Plasticine-type modeling clay

Fig. 40-1 Wibble-Wobble.

MEASURE, MARK AND MAKE

1 Have a look at the project picture (FIG. 40-1) and the working drawing (FIG. 40-2), and see how the Wibble-Wobble is put together and decorated. Note how the plaster holds the lead shot, and how the dowel links the two balls.

2 Use an old pencil to make a hole in each of the Ping-Pong balls. Don't try to stab the holes with one great thrust, much better to ease the pencil in with a few little-by-little pushes (FIG. 40-3 top left).

Continued

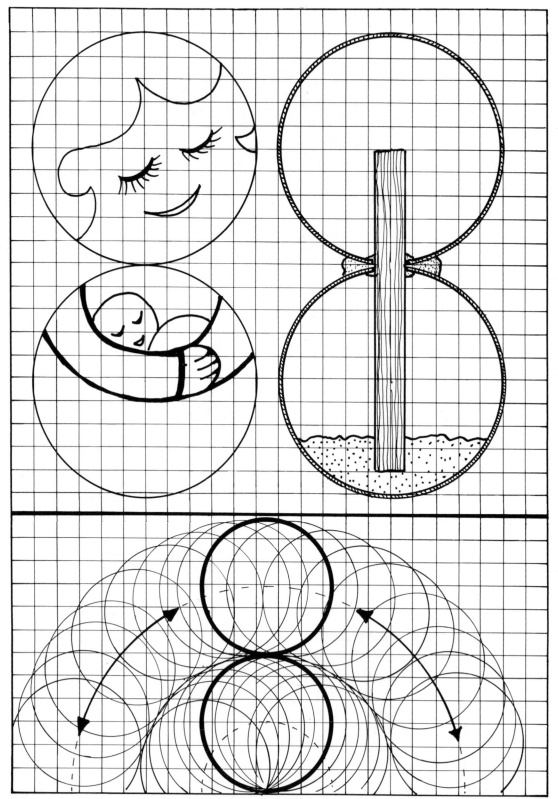

Fig. 40-2 Working drawing. Scale of top portion is about 3 grid squares to ½ inch. Scale of bottom portion is about 1 grid square to ¼ inch.

3 Support one of the Ping-Pong balls in a ring of Plasticine and pour the lead shot into the hole (FIG. 40-3 bottom left).

4 Cut a small nick in one end of the dowel.

5 Mix a small amount of plaster in a throwaway tub, pour the plaster in on top of the lead shot, and push the nicked end of the dowel down through the hole and into the wet plaster (FIG. 40-3 bottom right).

6 When the plaster is hard, squeeze a generous worm of clear quick-set glue around each of the holes—meaning around the dowel—and push the two balls together (FIG. 40-4 top).

7 When the glue is dry, use the brushes and the acrylics to paint in the colors that make up the design.

Continued

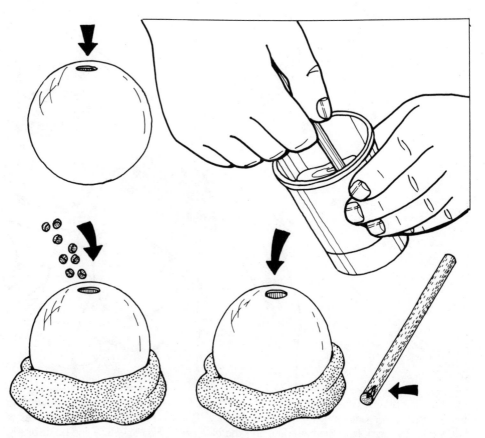

Fig. 40-3 (Top Left) Make a hole large enough to fit the piece of dowel. (Bottom Left) Support the ball with modeling clay, pour in the lead shot. (Right) Mix the small amount of plaster in a disposable container, pour the plaster into the ball, and push the dowel right down into the plaster. Allow to set.

8 Finally, when you have blocked in the large areas of color, say, black for hair, pink for skin, and blue for the dress, use the fine-point brush to pick out the details. You could have black for the features, red for the lips, and so on (FIG. 40-4 bottom).

WATCH-POINTS AND FOLLOW-UPS

○ When you are making the holes, be very careful that the balls don't split wide open. Support the balls in a ring of plastercine, so you won't hurt your hands.
○ Double-check that the glue is plastic-friendly.
○ When you are pouring the lead shot and the plaster into the ball, make sure that the level stays below the halfway mark of the ball.

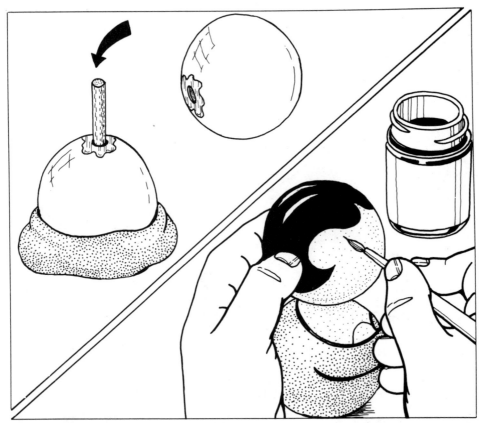

Fig. 40-4 (Top Left) Glue around each hole. Thread the second ball over the dowel and push it firmly down onto the first ball. Leave to dry. (Bottom Right) Paint the large areas of colors first: the black hair, the pink skin, and the blue dress. Finally, with a fine-point brush, paint the features with black paint and the lips with red paint.

Glossary
Tools, technique, materials, and safety precautions

How many tools does a crafter need? Are the tools safe? Can you use alternatives? Beginners sometimes find that it's all a bit of a problem. Well, not so with this book, because our glossary will answer most of your questions. Best select a project, check the tools and materials list with the glossary, read the project through, have a look at the watch-points and follow-ups at the end of the project. If you still have problems, ask an adult.

acrylic paints A plastic PVA, easy-to-use, water-based, quick-dry paint. Acrylics are the perfect paint for kids' crafts. They can be used straight from the tube or tin, they are completely safe and nontoxic, and the colors are really beautiful.

adult help It's always a good idea to talk the project over with an adult. Tell them what you want to make, ask their advice, make sure they don't mind you using such-and-such a tool, and generally ask them to give you the go-ahead.

Aida cloth An open-weave fabric designed especially for cross-stitch-type embroidery.

beads Crafters need as many plastic and wooden beads as they can find. Beads can be used for "eyes" for washers on thin wires, for weights, and for wheels. They have hundreds of uses. Best to ask around and to start a collection.

bodkin A large blunt-point needle. Perfect for passing cords and twines through difficult holes and eyelets, and for sewing thick fabrics. When you are using needles and bodkins, always push the needle through the card or fabric so that the point is heading away from your body. Watch out for younger brothers and sisters and for pets.

brushes Brushes come in all shapes and sizes. Get yourself two good long-haired artist brushes, a broad point for painting in large blocks of color and a long, sharp fine-point brush for picking out details. Keep them clean and store them point-up.

card and cardboard General terms for all the stiff cardboards and containers. Look out for good, stiff card packaging, for breakfast cereal boxes, and for boxes and crates from electrical shops. If you have a choice, best to use cardboard that is plain on both sides.

compass or a pair of compasses A two-legged instrument used for drawing out circles and curves. Get a big pair with a screw-turn adjustment.

coping saw A small, safe, inexpensive, easy-to-use, fine-bladed saw used for cutting out thin section wood. Good for cutting holes, tight corners, and curves.

corks Crafters need corks for wheels, washers, weights, buffers, soft points, and so on. Ask around and save the long straight-sided corks from wine bottles.

cotton reels See *thread spools*.

cotton thread Best to use a natural cotton thread because it can be dampened, stretched, and knotted, and then dried and tightened.

crayons and markers There are all sorts of pencil crayons, wax crayons, and water pencil markers. I like using traditional wood-covered pencil crayons.

crepe paper A thin, strong, stretchy, crinkly, bright-colored paper, a bit like tissue paper. Good for paper decorations and for masks.

cross-stitch An easy-to-do embroidery technique. A colored thread is taken in-and-out a piece of Aida fabric to make a cross. The whole design is made up of little lines, squares, and crosses.

double-sided sticky tape A very useful clear-plastic sticky tape that is sticky on both sides. Perfect for joining card-to-card and wood-to-card, it makes for a strong nonmessy fixing.

dowel Meaning just about any smooth wooden rod. We use everything from pencil stubs to bits cut from broom handles.

drill I like using a hand-operated drill. It's safe, totally controllable, inexpensive, quiet, small, handy, and easy. A hand drill is a good tool for kids.

fold-tab clips Small brass pivotal clips used for fixing paper-to-paper and card-to-card. You just punch holes, pass the tabs through the holes, and bend them back on themselves.

felt-tip pens Felt-tipped or felt-nibbed pens are usually sold in multicolored packs. They are easy-to-use, safe, nontoxic, and really good for a quick-instant effect.

glue and adhesives There are so many glues and adhesives about; you really need to decide just what it is that you want to stick before you go shopping. We use white PVA glue for most jobs and clear quick-set balsa glue for instant gluing.

glue stick A stick of glue or adhesive contained in an easy-to-use "pen-" or "lip-stick-"type container.

masking tape Also call draughting (or drafting) tape or even stencil tape. A cream-colored sticky tape, good for holding parts together while you are working, and for all the other strapping, clamping, and fixing jobs.

hammer You need a small, lightweight hammer; best to get one described as a "4-ounce ball peen."

matchbox Little wood and cardboard matchboxes are very useful. You can turn them into containers for all your bits and pieces, you can stick them together for projects, and so on. Ask around and start a matchbox collection.

multicore plywood A thin, white-faced plywood that is made up from very thin layers of wood. Multicore is strong; it can be cut with a small saw, and it can be easily sanded down to a completely smooth finish.

paper punch A small tool used for punching neat, round holes. We use little hammer-tap tube punches and multisize punch pliers; both types are easy and safe to use.

pencil   You need a couple of good pencils; best get a soft 2B for tracing and a hard 2H for pencil-press-transferring.

pliers   Although you can manage with a pair of ordinary blunt-nose pliers, most of the tasks will be much easier if you get yourself a small pair of long-nosed combination wire snips and pliers.

prototypes   A small working model made just before starting the project for real. So, for example, if you aren't quite sure how, say, the glider is going to work out, all you do is to make a very speedy mock-up with scrap materials. You might decide to make changes to the design.

putting together   The last part of the project when you come to putting all the separate bits and pieces together. You might need a bit of extra help at the putting-together stage.

safety   Although all of the projects in this book have been carefully designed to avoid the use of dangerous tools and large pieces of difficult-to-use equipment, you will, of course, still need to use small, everyday items like scissors, needles, and pins. You always have to be careful: pins need to be counted out and counted back in again, scissors should only be used and held correctly, knives should only be used when an adult is helping, some glues and adhesives are a bit tricky and should only be used when there is an adult around, and so on. *All tools and materials are potentially dangerous!* Do you know that even a piece of paper can give you a nasty cut? Always talk to an adult before you start a project.

sandpaper   Sandpapers or glasspapers are best purchased in graded packs. You need a pack containing sheets that range from ''coarse'' to ''smooth.''

saws   You need two saws, a small flexible-bladed ''coping saw'' for cutting out thin plywood shapes and for cutting out curves and holes, and you need a small straight ''dovetail'' or a ''tenon'' saw for cutting through larger section strips and dowels. Always ask an adult before you use a saw, and when you do get to use one, go at it slowly and carefully!

scalpel or craft knife   If a project tells you to use a scalpel or craft knife, ask an adult before you start.

scissors   Every crafter needs a couple of pairs of scissors; you need a large pair for cutting out large pieces of card, and a small sharp-point pair for cutting out tricky details.

stapler   A small inexpensive paper-fixing machine. The small U-shaped wire clips are punched through the paper and bent over so that the sheets of paper or thin cardboard are held together; it's a very useful tool.

sticky tape   Crafters need sticky tape. It's easy to use, it's speedy, and it's non-messy. Get yourself a roll of clear sticky tape, a roll of masking tape, and a roll of double-sided sticky tape.

thread spools   Empty sewing thread spools are really good for wheels, washers, and weights. See if you can find the old-fashioned wooden kind. If not, you can use plastic or styrofoam ones.

throwaway containers   Crafters always need to be on the lookout for useful containers. There are matchboxes, plastic food drums, empty tin cans, plastic and foil packagings, wooden fruit crates, cardboard boxes, and so on; they are all very useful.

tissue paper   A thin paper for decorations, tissue papers come in all sorts of colors, qualities, and strengths.

tracing and tracing paper   You need lots of tracing paper—meaning a strong see-through paper. When you come to "pencil-press-transferrring" the order of work is as follows: make a careful tracing with the soft 2B pencil, outline the back of the tracing with the 2B pencil, turn the tracing right-side-up and fix it to the working surface (meaning the wood or cardboard), and finally go over the traced lines with the hard-pointed 2H pencil.

wire   You will need a little stockpile of odds and ends of wire. We use throwaway wire coat hangers, short pieces of copper wire stripped out of electrical cables (bits and pieces of old discarded cable that you might find in the junk box), and straightened-out paper clips. Ask around and see what's available.

working drawing   By "working drawings" we mean all the scaled and gridded drawings that lead up to the project. When you come to making a project, decide how large you want your project to be, then transfer the design square-by-square. Note: our grids are only rough guides; in most cases, the size of your "found" cotton reels, food drums, or whatever will more or less set the size of your project.

workout paper   Crafters need great piles of rough workout or scrap paper and cardboard. Ask around at local printers and stores and start a collection.

Index